When You Find *Another*

a conversation
about friendship...
among friends

When You Find Another

a conversation
about friendship...
among friends

Kay Harms

along with contributing friends

Ordering Information:

Special discounts are available on quantity purchases by churches, ministry groups, educators, and others. For details, contact the publisher at kay@kayharms.com.

U.S. trade bookstores and wholesalers: Please contact the publisher at kay@kayharms.com.

For more information about the author or other publications by the author, please visit her web site at www.KayHarms.com.

for

Michelle—

who first inspired me to write this message—

and my other

golden apple friends

Contents

Preface - When You Find Another...
Invite Her

After almost four full days of enjoying the Great Smokey Mountains with two of my oldest and dearest friends, we traveled home commenting that we had "solved all the world's problems." We had circled every imaginable subject with lively conversation.

Isn't that one of the things we all enjoy most about our friendships? Long, productive and easygoing conversation? Guys may feel closest to those they enjoy activity with, side by side getting the task done. But we gals love to sit leisurely across from one another, look into each other's eyes, occasionally touch the other's hand *and talk it all out*.

That's why I invited other women to join their sweet voices to mine in writing this book. I wanted to create a true conversation—the kind you enjoy with girlfriends over coffee. And I didn't want to dominate the conversation, but simply to facilitate it.

Some of the contributors are indeed close friends of mine. But many more are women I've "listened to" while sitting in my pajamas, sipping my coffee and reading their blogs on the Internet. All of them are women who have felt called to minister to women like you and me, whether through teaching Bible study classes, leading women's ministry groups in their churches, encouraging women through their blog posts, speaking at retreats and conferences or counseling women one-on-one.

Most importantly, these are women who have known the joys and pitfalls of friendship. You will find they generously share their hearts and gently bare their wounds while speaking with authenticity and grace.

And now I invite you to join the conversation. Yes, you can speak up, too. Use the optional study guide in the back of the book to facilitate discussion about the book with a group of friends. Also, I encourage you to visit the contributing authors' blogs or web sites if they have one listed. They would enjoy hearing from you.

Part 1

Let's Get the Conversation Started

Chapter 1 - Let's Talk about Friendship

What is a friend?

Friends are just those people who happen into our lives by circumstance and we end up going to a few lunches and calling on each other for favors, right? Well, maybe. But let's see if we can get to the root of this relationship so we're more likely to grow them healthy, sweet and strong.

A friend is someone who speaks into your life, and you speak into hers on a *mutual* basis.

A teacher and a student are not friends. The teacher speaks into the student's life, and the student must raise her hand to gain permission to address the teacher. This is not a mutual relationship.

A doctor and a patient are not friends. The doctor speaks wisdom and information into the patient's life and the patient pays the bill.

And make no mistake about it; a parent and a child (at least during the formative years) are not friends. The parent speaks into the child's life and the child listens. Later, when the child is older, the parent (hopefully) allows the child to begin speaking into her life and she begins to speak a little less into the adult child's life. Thus a friendship forms...gradually...at the right time.

A friend is one who speaks into your life and you speak into hers on a mutual basis.

"Friendship is to be purchased only by friendship. A man may have authority over others, but he can never have their hearts but by giving his own." --Thomas Wilson

What does friendship look like?

If friends are two people who mutually speak into each other's lives, **then friendship is an ongoing conversation**.

The conversation between friends is made up of:

- everyday chatter
- mutual silence
- deep and meaningful verbal explorations
- questions and answers
- pouring out of deep waters
- listening
- body language
- touch
- facial expressions
- shared activity
- laughter
- tears
- companionship
- time
- gifts
- actions
- and even separations

Can you think of other elements of the ongoing conversation between friends I've overlooked?

The conversation isn't just made up of words vocalized and heard or written and read. The conversation is everything two friends say to one another...through their words and their silence, their actions and their inaction, their intentional communication and their unintentional messages, their shared emotions and the hiding of their emotions. And the beauty of friendship is that every conversation looks different, sounds different, *feels* different.

The loveliest friendships of all feed our souls with the sweet and beneficial conversations they provide. They encourage us and push us forward to be all God created us to be. They comfort us and restore our souls when we feel broken, wounded or weary. They make us laugh and bring us joy. They remind us of who we are and *whose* we are and why we are who we are. And they give us faith and courage to keep on going.

Do friends only speak "good" into each other's lives?

Perhaps it's because the word "friend" sounds so, well, *friendly* that we assume that all that is spoken between true friends is good and sweet and kind and gentle and right. But the truth is friends do not always speak "good" into each other's lives.

Friends get angry and say things they later wish they could take back. Friends sometimes say the first thing that enters their minds, thus neglecting to filter out the hurtful, the unnecessary or the unholy.

In Psalm 55, David bemoaned to the Lord that he was distracted and restless because of the voice of his enemy. But the enemy was in fact a friend.

"For it is not an enemy who reproaches me, then I could bear it; nor is it one who hates me who has exalted himself against me, then I could hide myself from him. but it is you, a man my equal, my companion and my familiar friend. We who had sweet fellowship together, walked in the house of God in the throng."
(Psalm 55:12-14)

Friends do not always speak "good" into each other's lives, but true friends, godly friends, will certainly try.

And that's where this little book comes in. *When You Find Another* is an invitation to consider the quality and the health of our friendships. You may find a few inspiring and sweet tasting quotations sprinkled in the conversation, but the purpose of the book is to challenge us, to speak truth to us and to motivate us to action, so that we intentionally cultivate sweet, healthy friendships.

Why take friendship so seriously?

Former First Lady Barbara Bush said, "You don't just luck into things as much as you'd like to think you do. You build step by step, whether it's friendship or opportunities."

Many of your casual friendships may have happened by circumstance or whimsy, but if you want to cultivate spiritually beneficial, solid and enduring friendships it takes three essentials:

- courage
- initiative
- and personal responsibility.

While this book is a call to act with courage and take initiative with your friendships, it's predominantly a guidebook for how to take personal responsibility as a friend. We can continue to let friendships just develop "naturally," like sour apples on a wild apple tree, or we can cultivate blessed relationships that benefit us and our friends like sweet delicious apples in a well-tended orchard.

Let's talk about the different varieties of friendships.

Chapter 2 - Red Delicious Apple Friends

In the 1980s, Red Delicious Apples represented three-quarters of the apple harvest in the state of Washington. A decade later, reliance on the Red Delicious cultivar had helped to push Washington's apple industry to the edge financially. They just had too many of the bright red fruits in their baskets. As a result, in 2000, Congress approved and President Bill Clinton signed into effect a bill to bail out the apple industry, which had lost 760 million dollars in the previous three years due to over production of Red Delicious Apples.

The bottom line? Red Delicious Apples are sweet and good, but they're also common and abundant. There is no great demand for them, but they seem always to be available.

If you're like me, you probably have a large number of friends who would fall into the category I've (lovingly) labeled Red Delicious. While I would hesitate to call these pals common, they are the brand of which we have the most.

If our friendships are defined and categorized by the ongoing conversations we have within those relationships, these Red Delicious friendships are marked by the more ordinary conversations with others. Just as there are 42 different mutations of the Red Delicious Apple, we can have dozens or even hundreds of different adaptations of Red Delicious Apple friendships.

My hairdresser, Marilyn, has been cutting and coloring my hair for about eleven years. We hit it off from the very beginning, even though Marilyn and I do not share multiple commonalities. She is not religious at all and I am a devoted follower of Christ.

She is a native Arizonan and I am a Georgia peach. She is in her 60s and I'm a decade behind. And we undoubtedly cancel each other's votes out in every political election.

But one thing Marilyn and I do have in common is that we are both mamas. And while our kids are not the same ages, nor do they even know each other, together Marilyn and I have walked our children through middle school, high school, dating, college preparation, scholarship applications, the college experience and those first jobs. Once every two months Marilyn and I spend a good hour or more talking nonstop about our children. Other than Daniel, Abigail, Wendy and Leslie, we don't have much in common. But we've spoken volumes into each other's lives in the area of parenting. Marilyn is a Red Delicious Apple friend.

C.S. Lewis wrote, "Friendship is born at the moment when one person says to another, 'What! You, too? I thought I was the only one!'"

Red Delicious Apple friends are your "another" friends: *another* woman who writes, *another* woman raising a child with special needs, *another* knitter, *another* mother of preschoolers, *another* empty nester, *another* woman training for a marathon, *another* hiker, *another* military wife, *another* avid reader.

The seeds that bring forth Red Delicious Apple friends are simply the commonalities we share. Do you have Red Delicious Apple friends? Sure, you do! You know them from work, the soccer field sidelines, your daughter's ballet studio, the gym, the parent-teacher organization, the yarn shop, your church, your book club, your pottery class or the marching band booster club.

Can you have too many Red Delicious Apple friends?

Washington had too many Red Delicious Apples and the abundance got the industry into harsh financial straits. But, unless you gather Red Delicious friends to the exclusion of any of the other varieties I'm going to share with you, I don't think you can ever have too many of these "another" friends.

Why is that? These are the friends who present you with the opportunity of sharing the love of Jesus with the world. While Marilyn and I talk mostly about our children, I do freely speak into her life about how I pray for my children, how I base my parenting on the Bible and how God works in my family's lives. If we Christ followers don't bother to find our "anothers" and "pick them" as friends, we tend to insulate ourselves in the cocoon of Christianity and we miss opportunities to build relationships in which we can share the gospel.

What if your basket isn't full of Red Delicious friends?

Because I live in a military town where people come and go like a game of fruit basket turnover, I occasionally realize that my Red Delicious Apple friend list has been depleted, at least locally. And life just isn't as sweet without a bountiful basket of Red Delicious Apple friends! Wouldn't you agree that these are the friends you enjoy sitting with at your child's sporting event, hanging with at your husband's office party, commiserating with at the parent-teacher meeting or gaining insight from at the yarn shop? So if I want to keep a bountiful supply of these fun-to-know friends I have to get out there and "make some!"

Here's the call for personal responsibility, initiative and courage.

For years I lamented the fact that no one ever invited me to lunch or the movies. "No one sat beside me at the meeting." "No one invites me to go shopping." Didn't anyone want to be my friend?

Then I remembered what my mother, a master friend to so many, taught me as a young girl:

To have friends, be a friend.

It's time to stop waiting on friendship and create it instead. Find friends. Search for friends. Befriend friends.

Here's my simple remedy for making new friends. It requires courage, persistence and vulnerability. (And it will clue you in to the title of this book, too.)

When you find another, invite her.

When you find another woman who shares your interest or unique life path or pursuit or season of life, *invite her*:

- to lunch
- for a walk
- to a museum
- to sit with you at the game
- to play a round of golf
- to discuss a book
- to ride with you to the meeting
- to do just about anything and everything you have in common with your "another!"

So repeat that back to me: *When you find another, invite her!*

When I began assembling this book I noticed that many fellow bloggers had interesting and profound things to say about friendship. I only knew a handful of them personally, but I plunged forward and extended an invitation to join me on the common ground of compiling a book on a topic we mutually deemed important.

Assuming I would receive a positive response from perhaps as many as one fifth of those I invited, I was caught off guard when almost 99% of the women I asked said yes. And those who declined simply couldn't contribute due to previous commitments and heavy workloads. In the same way that my fellow writers eagerly accepted my invitation to join this book's conversation on friendship, I think you'll find that many women will welcome your invitation to join in the activities of your life. There's just something about receiving an invitation. Don't you get a kick out of being invited to join someone else for...anything? Sure you do. We all love being thought of, considered, anticipated and included.

Still, so many of us fail to offer invitations. Instead, we wait to be included. We focus on that which we weren't invited to rather than creatively planning opportunities for including other women in our lives. Or, if you're like me, you keep a tally. Maybe you extend an invitation. She accepts. You both enjoy. Then what? You wait a while and nothing happens. If you're determined and resilient, you invite again. She accepts. You both enjoy...again...even more. And, once again, you wait. Nothing happens. Do you invite again? Hmm. It's a daunting proposition, isn't it?

Look, I feel your angst. The other women who have contributed to this book surely do, too. We've all reached our quota of extended invitations at some point only to notice that we've received nothing in return. That is, indeed, frustrating.

Allow me, however, to let you in on a little secret. *The sweetest, dearest friendships I have ever experienced all began with one woman (usually not me, but the other) pressing in more than the other.* Someone has to press in. Someone has to decide this relationship is worth a little awkwardness, a little perseverance, a little humility. I'm so very grateful for the women who pressed in when I backed away shy. I'm thankful for the women who asked again when I first said no. I'm thankful for the women who kept offering until I finally got the hint and offered back.

You and I can be that kind of woman, too. We can be friendship initiators. It will take moxie and vulnerability, but what a gift our perseverance will prove to be when that initial invitation eventually leads to an enduring friendship.

So what are you going to do? *When you find another, invite her.* That is the charge to repeat in your mind when you're looking for a friend. It's your responsibility. Take the initiative. *When you find another, invite her.*

The problem with Red Delicious Apples

I don't eat a lot of Red Delicious Apples, do you? I prefer some of the newer varieties when I'm looking for a juicy, crisp fruit to round out my meal. One of the reasons I don't usually purchase Red Delicious Apples is because they "go bad" easily. Wouldn't you agree?

The same is true of Red Delicious Apple friends, unfortunately. They bruise easily. Maybe it's because we have less invested in these relationships so we don't protect them as well. Maybe it's because these folks are not always people we see eye to eye with on many levels to begin with. Or maybe it's just the frailty of human nature. But Red Delicious Apple friendships are easily damaged.

Have you ever had a Red Delicious Apple friendship go bad due to any of these common pests, bruises or diseases?

- jealousy
- gossip
- criticism
- husband bashing
- hurt feelings
- broken trust

I have.

Here's the call to personal responsibility. If I have a friendship that has gone bad due to mishandling—on my part or hers—it benefits me to step up to the plate, take at least my share of the responsibility and do all I can to polish that friendship back to its original sheen. Why? Because the cause of the gospel and the reputation of my God are at stake.

If I am a Christ-follower, I am obligated to treat my "another" friends according to His standards. And in case there's any question about those standards, the Bible tells me exactly how to treat my "anothers."

- Love one another (John 15:12)
- Outdo one another in showing honor (Romans 12:10)
- Live in harmony with one another (Romans 12:16)

- Serve one another (Galatians 5:13)

- Be humble with one another (Ephesians 4:2)

- Be gentle with one another (Ephesians 4:2)

- Be patient with one another (Ephesians 4:2)

- Bear with one another (Ephesians 4:2)

- Forgive one another (Ephesians 4:32)

- Encourage one another (1 Thessalonians 5:11)

- Build up one another (1 Thessalonians 5:11)

- Pray for one another (James 5:16)

- Look out for one another's interests (Philippians 2:3-4)

- Don't envy one another (Galatians 5:26)

- Don't grumble against one another (James 5:9)

And there are more where those came from.

Red Delicious Apple friendships bruise easily, but it's my responsibility to keep them healthy and sweet so that I can freely share the love of Jesus with those friends.

As we draw this conversation about Red Delicious Apple friendships to a close, I'd like to encourage you to consider how you treat those "another" friends. Don't look at the whole bushel and try to examine them; instead, take a closer look at just one or two of those sweet gals with whom you share something in common. Look over the list of scriptures that describe God's standards for our "one another" relationships and examine your chosen friendship(s) in light of those commands.

Finally, let's pray together for the personal responsibility, courage and initiative to make and keep truly beautiful Red Delicious friendships—the kind in which we can easily and frequently share God's love and grace.

Lord, You are generous to provide other women with whom I can enjoy so many facets of life. Sometimes those friendships form easily and effortlessly, but more often than not, I must work to cultivate the kind of friendships that endure. Give me the humility to initiate, the courage to persevere and the personal responsibility to ensure that each friendship I begin stays sweet and full of your love. Show me if any of my friendships are characterized by envy, grumbling, selfishness or impatience. Help me instead to treat my friends as Your Word commands, with love, gentleness, service, encouragement and patience.

Chapter 3 - Green Delicious Apple Friends

I don't care much for Granny Smith Apples, do you? I love them for cooking or baking, but if you just bite into one you'll find it to be rather tart.

Interestingly, we all have friends we don't really care too much to spend time with either. That's right. You read that correctly. We each have a few friends we prefer not to be around for long periods of time. When I first heard that interesting little fact on a radio show, I was appalled. How could that be? Friends you don't really like to spend time with?

But it's true.

Have you ever met a group of friends, say women from your church group or neighborhood or book club, for dinner at a favorite restaurant? You know that when you arrive there will be a long table with two rows of chairs facing each other, right? Have you done that thing where you try to navigate where to sit based on where you think others will sit? You don't want to be difficult, but there are one or two people you just prefer not to be straddled with for the duration of dinner. Am I right or am I right?

Why would we have friends and even call them our friends, but not especially care to spend time with them? The answer goes back to the definition of friends. Remember the definitions?

A friend is someone who speaks into your life and you speak into hers on a mutual basis.

A friendship is a relationship in which both parties mutually speak into each other's lives.

And the type of friendship you enjoy depends on the ongoing conversation of the friendship.

Thus, a Green Delicious Apple friendship is one in which the conversation has *soured*.

Where did I get the term Green Delicious Apple friendship? It just so happens that there is a region in Canada where the Granny Smith Apple, that tart cultivar usually reserved for baking and cooking, is called none other than a Green Delicious Apple! Works for me...and for this book!

So what causes a friend to become a Green Delicious friend? Maybe they:

- talk too much
- talk too little
- talk too loudly
- talk about themselves too much
- talk about their perfect kid or perfect husband too much
- talk over you
- talk about things you prefer not to discuss

I have some Green Delicious Apple friends. And they are indeed my friends. They are lovely people with whom I have something in common. They are my "anothers," only they've become green and tart to my taste because of what they speak into my life.

Even Jesus had a Green Delicious Apple friend. You got it. Judas. Not only did Judas betray Jesus in the garden with a kiss, but he undoubtedly consistently spoke into Jesus' life that which was sour and distasteful. When Jesus and His disciples were at the home of Mary, Martha and Lazarus, after Jesus had compassionately raised Lazarus from the dead, out of gratefulness Martha served Jesus supper and Mary worshipped the Savior lavishly by pouring expensive perfume on His feet. While Jesus humbly received Mary's rightful act of gratitude and worship, here's how His friend Judas responded in His presence:

But Judas Iscariot, one of His disciples, who was intending to betray Him, said, "Why was this perfume not sold for three hundred denarii, and given to poor people?" Now he said this, not because he was concerned about the poor but because he was a thief, and as he had the money box, he used to pilfer what was put into it. (John 12:4-6)

Of course Jesus, knowing the hearts of all men, not only heard Judas' scathing and insensitive words, but He knew the heart with which he said them. Talk about sour words!

How to treat a Green Delicious Apple friend

Yes, Jesus had a Green Delicious Apple friend, one for whom He went out on a limb and befriended, one in whom He invested and one with whom He spent large amounts of time. But that friend spoke into Jesus' life that which was completely distasteful and undoubtedly served as a source of temptation more than once for Jesus.

And yet, how did Jesus treat Judas? According to Scripture we do not have any evidence that Jesus treated His less-than-sweet friend any differently than He did the others whom He trusted. Throughout the three years of Jesus' ministry, He treated Judas with kindness, respect, love, compassion and gentleness. In fact, in the Garden of Gethsemane, just after Judas betrayed Jesus with a kiss, of all things, how did Christ respond to him?

And Jesus said to him {Judas}, "Friend, do what you have come for." (Matthew 26:50)

Jesus did not casually discard His Green Delicious Apple friend. He lovingly treated him like a friend...to the end.

While it may be tempting to steer clear of our Green Delicious Apple friends, I believe Jesus would counsel us to do otherwise. I believe He would tell us to lean in instead of pulling away, and to follow His example with Judas.

I don't usually bite into a Green Delicious or Granny Smith apple to eat it as is, but I do stock them in my refrigerator, especially during the fall and winter months. Why? Because they're great for baking pies and cakes, or stirring into oatmeal. But if I use Green Delicious apples I always sweeten them up. I add sugar, cinnamon, honey or raisins to make the tart apples more palatable.

If I have a friendship that has soured because the conversation has gone bad, instead of discarding that friendship I need to take the responsibility for sweetening that ongoing conversation. I can sweeten a soured conversation several ways.

I can give a little grace. Abraham Lincoln once said, "I don't like that man. I'm going to have to get to know him better." To show grace means I put aside what I feel like I deserve or want out of the friendship and I focus instead on the other person and what they may need from me. Perhaps they just need someone to listen, to understand, to show compassion or to encourage them.

Grace changes things. It changes people and situations and conversations. In Luke 4:16-22 we discover that Jesus began His ministry by speaking words of grace, and the people were "speaking well of Him, and wondering at the gracious words which were falling from His lips..." Grace is indeed amazing.

I can also sweeten a soured conversation by speaking truth. I don't have to just grin and bear it if my Green Delicious Apple friend is using bad manners or behaving rudely toward me. I can lovingly speak truth to her and perhaps save her from destroying or risking other relationships as well.

Another way to sweeten a conversation is simply to listen. People are aching to be heard. Perhaps I am the only one who gives my Green Delicious Apple friend a listening ear. Instead of resenting this "privilege," I can truly thank God for the opportunity to minister in this way.

I can change the subject, gently but firmly. And if necessary, I can simply tell my friend that for the sake of our friendship it would be best for me if we didn't talk so much about...whatever it is she dwells on. But once again, grace is needed.

Finally, I can pray for my friend. No, don't just pray for her to change! Pray for God to bless her, for her to feel His presence and for her to find what she is searching for in Him.

Truthfully, we will find ourselves with a Green Delicious Apple friend in our basket of friendships now and then. Don't panic and toss it. Sweeten it with gracious conversation. Follow the example of our Lord and speak words of grace. And continue to call her "friend."

Chapter 4 - Golden Delicious Apple Friends

I love to tell the stories of how I met my very best friends, don't you? These are the women who have sweetened and nourished my life like no others. Not only have they stood the test of time, but they have proven over and over to be truly good for me, through and through.

Our histories are rich with accounts of how we came in and out of each other's lives and in again. Sometimes we knew from the moment we met that we were destined to be golden friends. Other times our bonds grew with time and, seemingly, chance.

The story of the Golden Delicious Apple

Around 1891, in rural Clay County, West Virginia, a young man of about 15 years was sent out into his father's pasture with scythe in tow to mow the field. The farm boy wrote the following account in his diary:

I was swingin' away with the scythe when I came across a little apple tree that had grown about 20 inches tall. It was just a new little apple tree that had volunteered there. There wasn't another apple tree right close by anywhere. I thought to myself, 'Now young feller, I'll just leave you there,' and that's what I did. I mowed around it and on other occasions I mowed around it again and again, and it grew into a nice lookin' little apple tree and eventually it was a big tree and bore apples. Now my dad later gave that piece of the farm in a trade to my brother, B.W. Mullins, and later still he traded the farm place to Uncle Anderson Mullins. Uncle Anderson had a brother-in-law named Gus Carnes, and one day Gus and Uncle Anderson Mullins decided to send some of the apples to the Star Brothers nursery to tell what kind of apple it was. And that was when the tree became famous and started the Golden Delicious apple line, for it was that tree that has produced every last one of the Golden Delicious apple trees that have ever grown anywhere. The Starks sent a man to look at the tree, just like you've heard, and they bought the tree and the ground for 30 feet around it, and eventually they fenced it. They were to get all the fruit from the tree, down to the last apple.[1]

But there is more to the story. The Stark Brothers nursery bought the exceptional tree and the plot of land on which it had grown for the then-golden sum of $5,000.00. In 2010, an Italian-led consortium announced that they had decoded the complete genome of the Golden Delicious apple, and it had the highest number of genes (57,000) of any plant genome studied to date.

The Golden Delicious apple is not just a sweet, golden, tasty piece of fruit. It is an unusual and rare breed, a highly sought after prize and a carefully protected cultivar.

The Golden Delicious friend is no less of a gem.

The story of the Golden Delicious Apple friend

Proverbs 25:11 says, "Like apples of gold in settings of silver is a word spoken in right circumstances." While all friends do not speak "good" into our lives all the time, there is a friend who consistently speaks the right word at the right time: the Golden Delicious Apple friend.

This treasured friend doesn't just speak what we want to hear

---

[1] https://en.wikipedia.org/wiki/Golden_Delicious

or that which is witty or profound or resonating either. She speaks that which is truly good for us.

And if a Golden Delicious Apple friend is one who consistently speaks good into our lives, then it stands to reason that a friendship made up of two such people is one in which "good" conversation is the normal. Do you have that kind of friendship? I hope so. And if you do, I hope you'll treasure and refine it even more after reading this chapter. But if you do not have such a friend, my prayer is for you to be blessed with one. For a Golden Delicious friend is truly a Godsend.

Some people have called a Golden Delicious friend a "soul friend" or a "spiritual friend." You see, she is not just your best friend, though she may well be. The Golden Delicious friend qualifies as such because she is one who consistently benefits you spiritually. Do you have such a friend? Are you such a friend to another?

Let's look at the qualities of a Golden Delicious friend by using the acrostic APPLES of GOLD.

APPLES

A - Asking the deep questions

Proverbs 20:5 says, "A plan in the heart of a man is like deep water, but a man of understanding draws it out." Golden Delicious friends are allowed and even encouraged to ask you the deep questions in search of the deeply buried answers. They know how to dig a little deeper in your soul so that you are not permitted to "get away with" being glib or shallow or dishonest.

Dee Brestin, author of *The Friendships of Women*, wrote, "When I talk to my closest female friends, I feel my soul being sunned and watered when they ask questions, drawing out the deep waters of my soul."

The need for an atmosphere of trust and confidentiality is of course implied, but when you have a Golden Delicious friend you allow her the ability to bring to the surface that which you would otherwise be tempted to keep hidden or dormant. The questions asked between such friends do not have to be invasive or rude, of course, but instead they should be gentle invitations to share more. What types of questions am I referring to?

- What are you thinking about?
- What has God been teaching you lately?
- What concerns have you had with your daughter away at college?
- How do you feel about your youngest starting kindergarten?
- What are your dreams and goals for this new year?
- How can I be praying for you right now?
- How have your daily quiet times with God been going?
- What is your biggest challenge or struggle right now?

The Golden Delicious friend simply has the courage and the compassion to press in a little deeper, oh so gently. Do you have a friend with whom it is common and acceptable to ask the deep questions and to answer them?

P - Praying

Golden Delicious friends pray for one another, but also *with* one another. In fact, praying together is often the pigment that makes this relationship so golden to begin with. One of my very best Golden Delicious friendships began gradually, but quickly, as my new friend and I knelt on my living room floor to pray together three days a week, still sweaty and red-faced after completing our three-mile run together.

How do you begin the sweet habit of praying with a friend? You *bravely* invite her to pray with you. Remember, much of that which is precious and priceless in any friendship will require courage on your part.

P - Perspective given

This rare friend helps you gain valuable perspective on the situations of your life. How? She speaks truth into your life. So if this woman is to be one who consistently speaks Godly wisdom into your life, she must be, by default, one who knows and spends time in God's Word.

When I was in high school I had a dear friend named Candy. In fact, we are friends today, be it a long-distance friendship.

Even during our teen years, Candy would show up in homeroom many a day with a folded piece of notebook paper containing several Bible verses written out in her distinctive handwriting. She had found them in her Bible the night before as she thought about whatever teenage dilemma I was going through at the time. Candy was (is) a Golden Delicious friend because she gave me God's perspective on my situations.

How do you feel about speaking biblical truth to your friends? Maybe you feel uncomfortable with the notion simply because you are nervous about handling the Bible accurately. Then simply follow Candy's example. You don't have to paraphrase or turn Bible verses into modern prose; just write a Bible verse of truth or encouragement out and hand it to her. Truth speaking which lends godly perspective is one of the highest callings of the Golden Delicious friend.

L - Listening

"Listening is a magnetic and strange thing, a creative force," said psychiatrist Karl Menninger. "The friends who listen to us are the ones we move toward, and we want to sit in their radius. When we are listened to, it creates us, makes us unfold, and expand."

Ah, to unfold and expand! The Golden Delicious friend is one who consistently gives us the freedom and the place to stretch out fully the cramped muscles of our dreams and regrets, our plans and our frustrations. And when we've been listened to by this safe and trustworthy friend, we are mobilized to move forward with confidence and peace, newly refreshed and re-energized for life.

How are you at listening, really listening? Do you listen with your heart, your mind, your body and your eyes? Do you listen without interrupting or attempting to solve the problem? This is a skill worth developing if you want to be a Golden Delicious friend.

E - Encouraging

To encourage simply means "to infuse with courage." While it includes the idea of coming alongside, it also entails pushing forward. A Golden Delicious friend is that friend who takes you by the hand, walks alongside you for a distance and then squares your shoulders and gives you a gentle push to get you well on your way toward your destiny.

Ralph Waldo Emerson wrote, "The glory of friendship is not the outstretched hand, nor the kindly smile, nor the joy of companionship; it's the spiritual inspiration that comes to one when he discovers that someone else believes in him..." Ah! Don't you just love that?

This rare friend doesn't just encourage you with her presence to stay the course; she also encourages you with her words to choose a new course, when necessary, or to climb a little higher than you were wanting to. She dreams dreams for you and with you.

To keep this practical, let's understand that this encouraging friend doesn't just spur you on toward lofty dreams and goals. She also encourages you to be and do your very best in the everydayness of life. She helps you be a better wife, mother, employee, Christian, minister and daughter. You are simply a better woman for having been her friend.

S - Standards set high

This is a relationship set on holy ground. Even if it wasn't birthed there (and some are not), this friendship becomes golden when it adopts golden rules. What rules? Here are some examples:

- no husband bashing
- no gossip
- no criticizing of others
- no foul talk
- no immoral activities

Sound like "no fun?" Don't be fooled. The enemy of biblical and healthy friendships would love for you to think that holiness will drain your relationships of every ounce of joy. But that's a lie from the pit of hell. When you establish holy parameters for your friendship you will actually find a greater freedom, a sweeter joy and a healthier intimacy.

When my friend Kim and I first became friends (on our sweaty knees in prayer!), I remember she was the one who bravely introduced me to the idea of setting some high standards for our new friendship. She suggested we stay clear of gossip, that we be forthright with each other and that we commit to never trying to upstage each other, thus ridding ourselves of the tendency to be jealous of one another. To be honest, I was shocked. While I had some fairly saintly friendships, none of them were really set up with any kind of rules. I had been used to friendships just developing freely, willy-nilly. But what she suggested made sense. And it has worked...for seventeen years.

I cannot type this one suggestion firmly enough: Be brave enough to insist on some holy standards for your friendships. You will be amazed at the results.

GOLD

G - Gracious

Proverbs 16:24 says, "Pleasant words are a honeycomb, sweet to the soul and healing to the bones." If our friendships are characterized by the messages we speak into each other's lives, the Golden Delicious friendship must be characterized by gracious words.

I'm not just referring to friends speaking sweet or even forgiving words to each other, however. This friendship, by its very nature, calls for something much more. These are two friends who have both experienced the grace of God through a relationship with Jesus Christ.

Truly, while grace is a rare commodity in high demand in today's world, there is only one source from which it can be obtained. Only God has grace to issue. He is a God of great grace. Then, once one has received God's grace, one can also give it to others. In fact, some have defined grace as God's Riches At Christ's Expense. Do you see how that definition implies (correctly) that grace always begins with God through Jesus Christ?

You may find sweet and good friends who do not know Jesus as their saving grace, but you will not have a Golden Delicious friend, a Proverbs 25:11 friend, until you link up with one who knows Him well. In the same way, you cannot be a Golden Delicious friend without experiencing the transforming power of Jesus in your life.

Do you know Jesus? Do you have a life-changing, life-saving relationship with God through His Son? Really, He is the very best friend of all, you know. Before you go looking for a Golden Delicious friendship or even a Red Delicious one, you can begin the most amazing friendship of all with the One who laid down His life for you.

"Greater love has no one than this, that one lay down his life for his friends." (John 15:13) Right after speaking those words to

His disciples, Jesus called them His friends. And then, shortly afterwards, He did indeed lay down His life for them...and for us.

If you would like to know more about how to begin a life-changing friendship with Jesus, I invite you to visit my website at www.kayharms.com and contact me through the contact form provided there. I'd love to share with you how you can experience the grace of God.

Golden Delicious friends give each other grace because they've experienced the graciousness of God through Jesus Christ.

O - Oasis

"My friends are an oasis to me, encouraging me to go on," wrote Dee Brestin. "They are essential to my well-being."

Do you have a friendship characterized by the "oasis effect?" She's the gal with whom you spend an hour in her presence and you feel rejuvenated enough to return home to the mayhem of family life. Since she gives you biblical perspective you can go to work the next day. Because she has asked the deep questions your soul has been sunned and refreshed. Because she really listens to you, you feel heard and understood. And because she has spoken truth to you and given you a gentle push in the right direction, you can move forward instead of retreating to a "dark place."

Proverbs 10:11 says, "The mouth of the righteous is a fountain of life..." Once again, the source of that life-giving fountain is the righteous One, Jesus. Let me suggest a little something. While it's fine to encourage or rejuvenate your friends with a shared mani-pedi, consider giving her Jesus, too. Give her His love, His grace, His truth or a prayer in His name.

L - Levity and laughter

Lest you think this friend is good for nothing but praying together and sharing Bible verses, let me assure you that the best of Golden Delicious friends are those who also make us laugh. This is a friendship characterized by joy!

Your Golden Delicious friend is not one you turn to only in times of despair or weariness or need. She is the one you enjoy being with most of all. And if you are to be a true and lovely Golden Delicious friend to others, you will need to learn to take yourself less seriously, to look at the bright side, to see the hilarious in the hellacious and to laugh, really laugh! Do you contribute laughter to your friendships?

D - Directional

Golden Delicious friends are, above all, two individuals headed in the same direction. They are focused on their relationships with God and are striving to live for Him. They are both walking the narrow path blazed by Jesus when He said, "Enter through the narrow gate; for the gate is wide and the way is broad that leads to destruction, and there are many who enter through it. For the gate is small and the way is narrow that leads to life, and there are few who find it." (Matthew 7:13-14)

Because Golden Delicious friends share the path less traveled, they have much in common, especially the core issues of life. Thus they don't get each other off course by suggesting deviant paths. Likewise, they are able to keep each other company on the narrow path when it seems like the rest of the world is marching to the beat of a divergent drummer.

While it is desirable to have friends who are different from us, unique, and even of varying faiths and backgrounds, the honor of Golden Delicious friend should be reserved for one who is walking with Jesus. That's the friend who will be there to pick us up when we stumble on this difficult trail.

Two are better than one because they have a good return for their labor. For if either of them falls, the one will lift up his companion. But woe to the one who falls when there is not another to lift him up. (Ecclesiastes 4:9-10)

How do you find a Golden Delicious Apple friend?

Maybe by now you have already identified one or two of your present friends as Golden Delicious friends. Or at least perhaps you see the potential or the making of such a friendship. Let me encourage you to value that friend, just as the Stark Brothers valued the Golden Delicious Apple tree enough to pay $5,000 for it at a time when that sum could buy a house or two.

Cultivate that friendship so that it grows into something truly beautiful, unique and beneficial to you both. Bravely ask the deep questions and, likewise, be courageous enough to answer them. Pray for one another and with each other. Offer only biblical perspective and not worldly advice. Listen to one another, really listen. Encourage your friend to be all she was created to be. Stand with her and walk beside her until she reaches her destination.

Set those standards high. That takes courage and a willingness to endure a little awkwardness. But it's worth it. I'll even offer you a "money back guarantee" on that one, for what that's worth!

Give each other grace, an oasis in your times of stress and lots of laughter, lots and lots of uninhibited laughter. But more than anything keep going in the same direction. Keep walking with Jesus, both of you, and the journey will be all the sweeter.

But if you realize you do not have this rare breed of friend, don't fret. First of all, let's understand that for most of us, if we can count one, two or three of these priceless Golden Delicious friends among those in our possession, we are rich, even ridiculously wealthy. And such friends do not come along just every day. Then again, they may pop up in the strangest places.

Still, I suggest that if you desire to find and cultivate a Golden Delicious Apple friend you go where they almost seem to grow on trees: the church. That's where I met my first Golden Delicious friend. Or at least, while we may have shared classes in school, it was at church that we realized we were walking in the same direction and needed the encouragement and support of each other. For over 40 years Michelle and I have spoken truth to each other, prayed together, encouraged one another and laughed together. And it all started in a youth Sunday school class. You could probably find a similar enduring friendship at Christian moms group, a women's Bible study class, choir or Christian exercise class.

But, besides looking for a Golden Delicious Apple friend at church, there are a few other things you can do to prepare yourself for such a friendship as well. First of all, pray for one. Ask God to send you a soul friend, a spiritual friend, a kindred spirit. At the same time, ask Him to create those APPLES of GOLD qualities in you, so you'll be ready when you find her. Then, begin being a Golden Delicious kind of friend to everyone in your basket of friends. Whether they are Red or Green Delicious, you treat them like gold! Pray for them, offer to pray with them, be an encourager, listen, ask deeper questions and keep their confidences, share truth in love and offer laughter and joy whenever you can.

Golden Delicious Apple friendships are rare beauties. They require time and tender care and, quite honestly, a little bravery on your part. But the promise of God's Word is that these are the friends who will do you the most good and grant you the opportunity to do them a little good as well. This golden friend is what the blessing of friendship is all about.

Chapter 5 – The Bad Apple Friend

Even a bad apple usually starts out sweet and appealing. But somewhere along the way the apple turns from shiny and red to bruised and brown. Something—disease, worms, bruising, age—causes the apple to lose its healthy benefits.

You may have had a friendship or two that came from bad seeds—unhealthy alliances or shared devious experiences. You know the kind I'm talking about. I'll be the first to admit I made a "friend" or two when I was somewhere I shouldn't have been or doing something I shouldn't have been doing.

But that's not the bad apple friendship we need to talk about. In fact, the bad apple friendship isn't one that goes bad because the *friend* is bad. More likely, she's just not good for *you*. And you're not good for her either. Individually you might even be golden and true, but together you're a toxic fruit cocktail.

The bad apple friendship is a codependent one. While codependency usually reveals itself quickly enough in familial and mentoring relationships, the codependent *friendship* often wears the disguise of BFF (best friend forever). In a day when it is popular to wear halves of jewelry that would spell out "Best Friends Forever" if they were pieced together, it's not so popular to address the downside of this distinctly female craze.

So just to set the record straight, I'm not insinuating that your very dearest friend is necessarily too invested in your life and you in hers. Instead, I'm confessing that that was the case in my own life...for fourteen years. I wouldn't admit it at the time if my life had depended on it, but it was true all along. We were in a sweet, but sticky relationship.

The Sweet and Sticky of Codependency

What does codependency look like in a friendship? Will I know if I'm in one?

Honestly, I knew from the very beginning of my co-dependent friendship that I was biting off more than I could chew. As we began to get to know one another...rather quickly, I might add...there was a thrilling sense that this could be dangerous. I was fascinated because I had finally found someone who seemed like a perfect match for me in so many ways. We enjoyed doing many of the same things, saw eye to eye on life issues, conversed enthusiastically and effortlessly about anything and everything, laughed together constantly and prayed together easily. Still, something didn't seem quite right.

The ease of our friendship drew us into a quick and deep intimacy. Early on in our relationship we shared personal struggles, deep regrets, hidden secrets and yet unspoken dreams, all with unbridled transparency. Feeling like we had each finally found our "kindred spirit", the mutual intimacy felt sweet and satisfying to both of us. Before we realized we were travelling ninety-to-nothing down a dangerous path, our hearts linked together with a sticky bond. Soon we no longer just *enjoyed* each other, we *needed* one another...to feel whole, secure, purposeful and happy.

> "Emotional dependency occurs when the ongoing presence and nurturing of another is believed to be necessary for personal security."
>
> – Lori Rentzel, *Emotional Dependency*

Having found all we needed from a friend in each other, my friend and I over-invested in our relationship and under-invested in others. Sure, we both had other girlfriends, but we were rarely fully present with any of them. Looking back, I realize that even if I went out to lunch with another woman, my BFF filled the empty chair at the table. Also my husband and children often had only my divided attention. But saddest of all, I failed to cultivate a deep and intimate friendship with Jesus because my "best friend" met all of my needs...or so I thought.

I hope you understand that this friendship was overwhelmingly sweet, but also undeniably sticky. It felt good, probably looked good to others and even produced some good things in our lives. Deeply invested in each other, we encouraged one another to pursue God-given dreams, prayed for one another devotedly and counseled each other wisely...as long as the wise advice didn't penalize or restrict our own friendship in any way

But while it felt mostly good, the friendship was unhealthy. It consumed each of us and drew us away from other people and pursuits. Most importantly, it quickly became an idol that we elevated before our individual relationships with God. *Instead of finding our identity in being His beloved, we found our identity in being one another's BFF.* It breaks my heart when I consider how this friendship surely grieved the Lord.

If you're in a friendship like the one I've described, my bet is that you're wrestling with this chapter and resisting the wisdom in it. I understand. I resisted the truth about my friendship for so many years. But sister, I do hope you'll prayerfully consider the list of toxic signs that I provide here. The enemy will convince you that giving up your sweet, sticky friendship will utterly devastate you. In truth, it *will hurt* at first. Because you have given too much of your heart to this one person, you may feel like you have lost a large chunk of yourself when you either step away from this friendship or even do the hard work of making it healthy. Still, you can and must break free from a codependent relationship. Otherwise you remain in bondage to something that *will* eventually destroy you.

The Stickiness Test

I encourage you to carefully and prayerfully consider your most intimate relationship with a person (other than your spouse) in light of the following assessment tool. Ask God to help you honestly evaluate each statement. Be brave enough to be truthful about what you discover.

Check each statement that is true.

____ I frequently feel jealous or possessive in this relationship.

____ I desire exclusivity in this relationship and see other people as threats to the friendship.

____ I'd rather spend time alone with this individual, and I become frustrated when this doesn't happen or others intrude.

____ I become hurt or depressed when this person withdraws even slightly.

_____ I have lost interest in other friendships and prefer this one.

_____ I spend a lot of time focusing on this friend's problems, interests or plans.

_____ I prefer not to make plans without consulting or involving this friend.

_____ I expect this friend to consider me at all times, even though I may not have verbally expressed this need to her.

_____ I do not easily see this friend's faults.

_____ I have made others uneasy with my familiar and intimate treatment of this friend.

_____ I talk about this friend often.

_____ I even "speak for" this friend at times.

_____ I am physically affectionate toward this person beyond what is generally considered appropriate for friends.

_____ I've been defensive about this friendship when others have asked or commented about it.

_____ I dislike being away from this friend for extensive time.

_____ I have secrets with this friend.

_____ My conversations with this friend often revolve around our feelings for each other.

(This list is based loosely on a similar list provided by Lori Thorkelson Rentzel in her pamphlet *Emotional Dependency: A Threat to Close Friendships*. San Rafael, California: Exodus International.)

Just to clarify, how does a healthy friendship contrast with the statements listed in the assessment tool? A healthy friendship can still be intimate and fulfilling, but it is characterized by:

- freedom and encouragement to invest in other *equally* close relationships

- respect for personal boundaries

- nurture and appreciation of separate identities and pursuits

- frequent inclusion of other people

- unquestioned freedom to withdraw or hold back

- pleasure in seeing the other succeed or be blessed separately

- respect for privacy and autonomy

- joy, identity and purpose *outside of* the relationship and which has nothing to do with the other person

What Now?

If you found that a few or more of the statements in the assessment tool described a current friendship, I compassionately suggest you take a long, hard look at the relationship. It's definitely difficult to take a step back from a friendship in which you have become so entwined, but it's necessary. Perhaps you could look over the list with another Christian woman who cares about you and who would be able to help you honestly evaluate your friendship. I realize that's a big step, but I have found there is amazing benefit in conducting all of my relationships out in the open. In the fresh air of accountability and transparency, my relationships can grow into what they were meant to be – opportunities for godly encouragement and joyful, sweet companionship – and nothing more.

From Sticky to Sweet Again

Is there hope for the codependent friendship? I can tell you from experience that you *absolutely can* create a safe, sweet and satisfying friendship from one that has become too sticky. However, it will take time, repentance, immense self-control, the involvement of other people, immersion in biblical truth and an act of God. Did I mention time? Well, I meant *a lot* of time. Oh, and that's time apart. *Not* time working through this together.

Actually, if you recognize yourself and your friendship in this chapter, I suggest you tell someone you trust immediately. Pray about it only long enough to decide who to tell, and then dial the number or walk into the next room and spill the beans.

You see, if you are in a codependent friendship you are robbing yourself and your friend of the true intimacy you are meant to have only with Jesus, our dearest friend. You are also cheating each other out of the opportunity to be fully who God created you to be individually. Your husband, children, other friends and co-workers rarely have your full and undivided attention. And you have undoubtedly become unfamiliar with your own inner voice, the one that expresses only *your own* hopes, dreams, opinions, preferences and longings.

> "Unless you know the truth about codependency,
> you can spend your entire life knowing something is
> wrong but thinking everyone else feels the same
> way. But, my friend, they don't."
>
> - Jan Silvious, *Please Don't Say You Need Me*

Ultimately, you need to be willing to sever the unhealthy friendship. Why? Because you (and she) are worth what may be gained only by walking away. However, if you want to try to salvage a friendship, one marked by freedom, individuality, devotion to your Lord and emotional health, I certainly encourage you to do the hard work that will be necessary. It took my friend and me almost three years of agonizing changes and extreme withdrawal from one another to develop a healthy and sweet friendship we are equally proud of, committed to and individually healthy in.

And I must be honest with you, some days that friendship looks and feels like a shell of what we once had. Some days it feels empty and unfulfilling and lonely. But that's only because we had *over-invested* before. Truthfully, even in the moments when our new friendship feels a little dissatisfying, I know that it is healthy and holy in God's eyes. It brings Him pleasure and allows Him alone to satisfy the soul needs we once tried to meet in each other. And because of that, I am closer to Jesus and more useful to Him. I want that for you, too.

Chapter 6 - What's in Your Basket?

So those are some of my thoughts on friendship. I love the analogy of apples when exploring the different types of friendships we have grown because, while the different varieties of apples all appeal to us differently and vary in popularity, they're all sweet and beautiful. They're little treasures that make life sweet and wholesomely good. Our friends do the same, do they not?

Now that I've shared my thoughts on friends and friendship, I'd love to hear your thoughts as well.

Will you help me out?

Often when I speak at conferences for women and girls, I speak about friendship. In a day when we work hard at accumulating Facebook friends and blog followers, I think it's important for us to take another look at the value of investing in day-to-day, person-to-person relationships. And God intends for friends to benefit us as we work out our faith in the real world. We're supposed to sharpen one another as Proverbs 27:17 says. And we're supposed to lift each other up, pray for one another, share one another's burdens and teach one another. We can best do that in the relationship we call friendship.

So as I continue to prepare a fresh word on friendship each time I speak to women about finding, creating and cultivating godly relationships with other women, would you help me by sharing your thoughts on friendship with me? Here's what I'd love to know.

- What do you find hard about making friends?
- How have you overcome the hurdles of making friends?
- What friendship "bruises" have you experienced and how did they affect you?
- When have you needed to be brave in a friendship? How did you act courageously?
- What frustrates you about friendships with women?
- What are the greatest joys of friendship you have experienced?

- If you've been in a toxic, sticky friendship, how did you get out or make it wholesomely sweet again?

If you would like to share answers to these questions or any other insights you have on friendship, I'd love to hear from you. Connect with me at www.facebook.com/official.kayharms/ or at my website kayharms.com. Feel free to email me at kay@kayharms.com, and I will definitely email you in return.

And Now, a Friendship Challenge

I'd like to spur you to action. Unlike a lot of great books I've read on friendship, this little book was not meant to be just a sentimental reflection on this powerful gift. It's meant to challenge you to keep your basket of friendships sweet and healthy, regardless of the varieties. So...

Red Delicious Apple Friend Challenge

Are there some bruises on any of your Red Delicious Apple friendships? Gossip, criticism, husband bashing? What do you need to do to polish these friendships to their intended glory? Why don't you jot down a few commitments in regards to one or more of these sweet friends?

Do you need to make some new Red Delicious Apple friends? Get out there, take the responsibility, be brave and... "When you find another, invite her!" You've probably already identified a few "anothers" you could invite to join you in a mutually enjoyable activity. Today, could you pick up the phone or message one through Facebook and invite her to do something with you this week, before you get swept up in the busyness of life? Do not wait for life to get more manageable or for your house to be in better shape; act now.

Green Delicious Apple Friend Challenge

Have you been avoiding a Green Delicious Apple friend because the conversation between you soured somewhere along the way? How might you sweeten it? Do you need to take some responsibility for the sour conversations and sweeten things up? Why not begin by praying for that friend right now? God will show you how to give grace if you ask Him.

Golden Delicious Apple Friend Challenge

Do you have one...or more? Thank the Lord, seriously! And commit to keeping those friendships on holy ground. What one characteristic of the APPLES of GOLD acrostic do you need to work on in your Golden Delicious friendship? Schedule a time to talk with her about it this week.

Do you lack a Golden Delicious Apple friend? Begin praying for one and about how to be one. Practice the traits of the Golden Delicious friends, and before you know it you may find yourself being one and having one. What one trait will you begin working on today?

Bad Apple Friend Challenge

Have you identified one of your friendships as both sweet and sticky? I understand the temptation to cling to it, and I know that it may feel almost impossible to change it. But you must.

If you are crazy-glued to your friend you must reconcile with the fact that you have constructed an idol. You have begun to go to her for satisfaction that only God can safely and sufficiently provide. You must learn to find your identity in Him and not in your friend. You must learn that His love is enough to fill your heart. You must learn that while intimacy with Him is completely safe and fulfilling, that kind of soul-baring intimacy with anyone else (other than your spouse) is dangerous and untrustworthy. It leads to bondage and eventual destruction.

Your challenge is to seek a Christian counselor who can wisely lead you out of codependency and into healthy relationships. Also, I'd like to recommend a book that helped me tremendously in this challenge. Jan Silvious' book *Please Don't Say You Need Me: Biblical Answers for Codependency* remains permanently in my Kindle library for occasional review. It's that good. (By the way, you'll get a kick out of the book's cover. I promise you I had already delivered this message numerous times and written the first few chapters of my book before I ever laid eyes on her book cover! But when I needed her message, the cover drew me in.)

Part 2

Let's Hear from Others

Because friendship is a conversation, I've invited a few other voices to join us. I know most gals like a story, so I invited a few personal friends and some of my cyber friends to tell us a story about a special friend or group of friends in their lives. I wanted to know how they met, what made them click, how their relationships sweetened over time and even why things eventually changed...if they did.

These gals were sweet to share their stories with us. And those who write regularly on the Internet have also shared their contact information. I hope you'll visit their websites.

Finding a Friendship Lost
by Valerie Sisco

I was a little mystified as I stared at the email sender's name in my in-box because I'd only ever known one person with the name Sammie. She was my best friend in second grade. And I hadn't seen her in forty years.

I still remember how my seven-year-old heart was broken when she moved away. It seemed as if Sammie had just joined my class in the middle of the school year, and now her family was moving again.

We were kindred spirits. We often played together while our mothers sat nearby talking. They chatted endlessly about their penchant for junk. Before it was reality TV-fashionable, Sammie's parents went digging for old bottles and vintage cast-offs in trash dumps and houses slated for demolition. These trash-to-treasure expeditions fascinated my mother who could never convince my father to do anything so unconventional.

We weren't friends for long when Sammie told me her family was moving again. This time they were off to Alabama. It might as well have been a million miles away from my home in Pittsburgh.

Before they left, Sammie's mother gave my mother a framed picture of hundred-year-old newspaper clippings that my mother had admired. Sammie's mother yanked the picture right off the wall and handed it to my mother, who protested but eventually accepted the gift.

I missed my best friend and wrote her a few letters. A year later my family drove for hours from our vacation in Florida for me to see Sammie in Alabama. We got lost and arrived so late that we spent a sleepy hour there before driving back to our hotel. I never saw her after that and we lost contact with each other.

But the newspaper clipping picture her mother had given mine always hung on the wall in our house as I grew up. One of the clippings had Sammie's brother's name, Tucker, in the headline, so every time I saw the picture I thought of her.

All of these memories flashed through my mind as I opened Sammie's email.

She said she had occasionally searched the internet for me and had just discovered that I was writing a blog. She said our childhood play dates were happy memories for her and she'd never forgotten my family's faith and how we attended church.

I was shocked to discover that we'd lived in the same Florida city for the past 25 years. We were just a few miles from each other, but almost a thousand miles from where we'd first met as schoolgirls.

We met for lunch a few weeks later and, as we hugged hello, we both admitted we were a little nervous. But it felt like we'd never lost touch.

Sammie was just a grown-up version of her second grade self. She was the same bubbly, full-of-life girl I remembered. We talked for three hours, catching each other up on our lives.

As Sammie told me she was sure God had brought me back into her life to encourage her in her faith, I was amazed at the design and detail of God's plans.

God took what was broken by time and scattered by distance. He gathered all the vintage pieces and relics from the past and restored them to a beautiful and treasured second chapter of friendship.

Valerie Sisco is a corporate writer living in Orlando, Florida, where she adorns her home with vintage treasures and flea market finds. She writes the blog Grace with Silk.
http://www.gracewithsilk.com

Letting My Guard Down
by Bridget Bareither

That particular summer brimmed full with more change than my heart could handle. Just two months earlier, my husband and I felt led to sell our condo in the Chicago suburbs. We weren't exactly sure why, since we had been at the same crossroads two years prior—sold our house, moved two hours from family and started over—and here we were again.

Our house sold within days of being put on the market. We moved in with family while we scrambled to find a new house in the transition, only to find out that my husband's company was offering him a promotion to move 850 miles away!

The whole series of events led me to a lot of "Why God?" moments.

"We just started planting our roots here! Why are You asking us to leave now?" I pleaded.

One of my greatest desires upon moving to the Chicago suburbs had been to find friends to do life with. I didn't want superficial friendships anymore. I longed for depth. Real, raw, vulnerable women to walk through life with. It was there that God had answered that prayer. He brought me genuine women who became a necessary glue in my life. For so long I had taken on the attitude of "I can take care of myself." But how wrong I had been. These girls were a blessing that I nearly missed out on!

On the days when my overly fussy baby was more than I could handle, a quick phone call and a desperate plea landed immediate help on my doorstep. When one of us needed a babysitter, another stepped in. When one of us just couldn't handle parenting alone that day, we organized a playdate. When one of our houses was a disaster, we helped each other clean.

I quickly realized that soon I would be leaving all this behind, that God was leading us to a new place. I would be alone...again.

Many tears were shed as we said our goodbyes and began our 850 mile trek. Reeling from the tender ache of leaving behind those who held my heart, I became fully aware that the only way I could meet new friends was if I let my guard down. A huge part of what had made these suburban friends so valuable to me was that they had helped me see that I was worthy of being loved. Time and time again they loved me selflessly without expectations. They showed me that real friendship is serving one another, loving unconditionally and just being there for each other.

Somehow we were able to find a church family immediately. One visit and we knew we were home. We desired a place for our family to grow in community, and we found that and so much more in this church. I joined a bible study and signed up for a moms group. I knew I needed to put myself out there if I expected to enjoy meaningful friendships.

The first few months brought wavering moments, both sad and lonely, but I pressed on and into the Lord. In the times I just didn't want to go anywhere, be with anyone or be forced to talk to others, I made myself go anyway.

Slowly, but surely, all the time and determination I had invested in meeting new people resulted in recognized familiar faces, offers for babysitting, invitations to coffee and a cherished girls' night. Each offer was affirmation: I am wanted. I belong. I am not alone. My efforts proved to be valuable investments in building the foundation for new friendships. As time went on, some of those friendships grew deeper. God gently showed me where it was safe to spread my roots.

In the moments I feared I would reveal too much, I would force myself to let go a little bit more. With time, more walls came down, crumbling with each act of vulnerability. Little by little, God created something new. Each moment with those friends seemed like God was reminding me that He knew my path and what or who I would need to travel it well. Eventually the "why, God?" moments became "thank you, God" moments instead.

Those friendships continued to blossom because I was willing to say yes even when I was afraid of letting my guard down. Even when I didn't know a single soul in a new place, He provided us a place to call home, a place to belong, a family.

Bridget Bareither is a wife and a mom to two littles. She is passionate about growing in her own relationship with the Lord and encouraging other women to do the same.

God-Gift Friendships
by Becky Keife

I don't even feel like I'm that same girl anymore.

Sometimes it's hard to remember that I was once her. That I spent two years lifting aching prayers for God to give me just one real friend to do life with. I was that desperate mom pushing my double stroller alone, scanning the park playground or library bookshelves hoping for a friendly face to connect with.

Making friends usually wasn't hard for me. I've always had quality women in my life. Women I love and admire. Women who know my story and I know theirs. But either life stage or geography had pushed these friends to the periphery. Now, in a season of juggling nap schedules for tiny tots, driving 45 minutes to see friends wasn't practical.

I needed a new inner circle. A day-in-day-out friend to walk through the ins and outs of motherhood together.

Oh, to have someone to make last minute plans with when fresh air and adult conversation were a saving grace to get through the day as a mama of littles.

Writing this induces memory tears from that deep place of longing that was once so real and searing. I cry for that floundering mom I used to be. For that Becky who yearned for meaningful friendships, but didn't know how to cultivate them in a new town with two (then three) little boys in tow. For that precious mama who just needed to know she wasn't alone.

Then I weep for the ways God *has* answered those longing-filled prayers. Answered them abundantly with incredible, beautiful, do-life-with friends.

Now my heart aches with the blessing. It actually hurts for how deep and wide God's love is for me. How lavishly He has poured out compassion, joy and grace through unexpected friendships.

I prayed for one.

God provided many...

- Desiree: My tell-it-like-it-is, purposefully doesn't clean before I come over with my crazy boy crew, brings me coffee creamer and chocolate, faithful friend. *I'm so thankful God brought us to the same moms' group table and knitted our hearts together through miles of sidewalk and countless coffee cups. There's no one I'd rather start my week with.*

- Audra: My laugh with, cry with, come as you are, loves me in my strengths and in my mess, all-is-grace friend. *I'm so thankful God sat us next to each other on a Sunday morning and gave me the courage to invite you over. I can't imagine these past years without you.*

- Mindy: My encourager, cheerleader, truth speaker, serves me with prayer and time and words, soul sister friend. *I'm so thankful God used a writing conference across the country to introduce me to my best friend down the street. You are a divine gift from God to me.*

- Elise: My interceding, dream believing, speaks the same heart language as me, kindred spirit friend. *I'm so thankful God used the Web to weave our paths together. You live 1,500 miles away but are always close to my heart. Your friendship is a heavenly answer to a prayer I thought had already been fulfilled.*

These gals are my prayer and play date friends. My call and text, unload with and be uplifted by friends. They love me well and they love my kids—a blessing words can't cover. They point me to Jesus, show me how to live by the Spirit and help me become more of the woman God created me to be.

These God-gift friends are soul beautiful. Authentic. Nonjudgmental. They are with me and *for* me. We share cooking tips, vacation books, hugs and tears and knowing looks.

These are my sisters.

My people.

Heavenly Father, thank You for hearing my cries and answering my prayers. Not meagerly, but extravagantly. Your Word says that every good and perfect gift is from above. These women are Your good and perfect gifts to me. My heart overflows with joy and gratitude for the work You have done. Blessed be Your Name!

Becky Keife is a writer, speaker, and blessed mama to three spirited boys. She is passionate about encouraging moms in the thick of it and shining light on God's fingerprints in her life. Becky also loves serving as Editorial Coordinator for (in)courage. Connect with her on Instagram @beckykeife or on her blog, www.beckykeife.com.

Transparency in Friendship
by Chris Adams

As a young mom I was heavily involved in serving in my church, trying to be the perfect mom, wife, servant, etc. But I set myself up for failure, since there are no perfect women.

When our twin girls were preschoolers, God brought into our church a precious woman who was about 15 years older than me and had teen girls. Both of us had families through adoption, so we had an immediate connection. She also had a heart for discipling women and for women's ministry, something dear to my heart.

We began a journey of what I thought would be primarily our working together, but God planned something much deeper.

If you met her today, you would immediately love her. And get this, her name is Delight! Of course it is! And she was truly that. I just assumed because she was so "Delight-ful" that her life must be perfect and, of course, her family must be perfect also.

Most women at that time didn't share deep hurts and painful experiences. Women of my generation and that of my parents were normally very quiet about tough issues in their lives, especially those within their families. But as we grew closer as friends in ministry, Delight was willing to share with me what her real life was like. I could hardly believe what she was sharing with me, and I didn't understand how she could be experiencing that kind of pain and still have joy and peace in her life. She continued faithfully loving and serving Christ through it all...never even doubting God's goodness and faithfulness.

I thought, *I could never do that*. Oh, famous last words, as they say! As my children grew, we began a journey similar in nature to Delight's family's journey. She was the first person I called because I knew she understood what I was experiencing as a mom. I also knew that if God could give her peace in the midst of it, He could give me peace as well.

We have journeyed now for many years together as friends (though I do not live close to her any longer) and as moms who love their children and want the best for them. Our journey has taken us on highs and lows, but we have both experienced God's faithfulness and strength. Our family, though still so far from perfect, has experienced some significant resolution and restoration. Her journey continues to have brokenness. But Delight still walks in faith, serving as an example to me of how a godly woman does life in the midst of confusion, pain, brokenness and disappointment. She has also shown me what it is to minister to another woman with authenticity and transparency, and how that becomes a lifeline to another woman.

My desire, as I benefitted from Delight's walk with Christ, was to become the same kind of example to other women as I shared my story and God's faithfulness with others. I can't imagine how I would have navigated life without her example. How great God is to give us Christian sisters to walk with us in life.

Chris Adams recently retired as Senior Lead Women's Ministry Specialist at LifeWay Christian Resources, Nashville, Tennessee. Prior to her employment at LifeWay in December 1994, Chris was the special ministries coordinator at Green Acres Baptist Church in Tyler, Texas. In 2008, Chris received the Career of Excellence award at LifeWay. She is a wife, mother of twin daughters and grandmother of seven. She also loves books, good coffee and chocolate!

Heartbreaking Needs, Heartwarming Friends
by Cindy Dykes

A family member was ill and I knew no one in a similar situation to whom I could turn. Doctors were doing all they could for the sick one, but I needed help for my spirit.

People did not understand. They could not relate. Mental illness was something to be shunned and silenced. I had spent months with the Lord asking how I was to respond to my loved one and who I should turn to outside of God and family. You would hope the church would be the answer, but more often than not I found Christians have the same attitude toward mental illness as the world. I was told, "Get this person in church and then God will take care of them" and "Tell your loved one to snap out of it." No one seemed to understand the illness or the situation...until I met Jan and Suzy.

I was in a meeting of women in our community who also dealt with family members devastated by mental illness. I was so relieved to find a place to say how lonely and sad I felt. I hoped this group was the answer, but it was not to be. When others heard the pastor's wife's story they gasped aloud and said, "I can't believe those things are happening in our pastor's home." I was devastated by their reactions to my honesty, but in that group of women was Jan.

Jan walked the same path I did. She did not treat me as anything but a friend in need. I did not go back to the group. Instead I began to lunch with Jan. Within a few months a new member of our church sought me out for friendship. Suzy was experiencing the same things Jan and I were. Glory! God had given me shipmates on the boat of suffering.

We began to meet every month for lunch and more often than not we spent the time laughing at our situations. I love how God can bring a light heart to heavy circumstances through sweet friendships. Our hour together became a time for lightening the heavy burdens each of us carried. The three of us were dealing with like circumstances and so we could freely speak, complain, cry and laugh without fear of reproach or a loss of privacy. We were hiking similar and difficult trails in life. God is so good. For the last ten years I have not walked alone, but had other women who shared my struggle and helped me carry my sorrows.

I love my relative who is ill. I love my friends who care and understand me. I love the Almighty Creator who keeps the earth in orbit and yet still took the time to make sure I was guided to friends who stand with me through tough times.

John 16:33 says, "…in Me you have peace. Be of good cheer (take heart!) I have overcome the world." I always see a smile and a sense of humor when it says, "take heart. I have overcome the world." In the midst of pain and difficulties there is a "take heart," and a chuckle amidst the tears with a hope in a Savior that cares.

Cindy Dykes has been married to David for 40 years. They serve the Lord together at Green Acres Baptist Church in Tyler, Texas, where David is the senior pastor. They have two daughters and four grandchildren. It is a busy time of life that requires a lot of humor as she works with four generations of her family daily.

When You Yearn to Belong
by Jennifer Jackson Linck

I remember peeking through the blinds and watching the group of girls next door. Their laughter was like a dagger to my heart. While they had fun, oblivious of the girl next door, I was alone in my room wondering why I didn't belong.

I questioned what was wrong with me.

I wondered why I hadn't been invited. After all, they were in my class.

And now, 20 years later, there are still times I feel like I'm on the outside looking in.

I've never been part of the in crowd.

My close friends have always been just one or two—and I'm grateful for them because they've endured the hard parts of life with me.

But there's still a part of me that wants so badly to belong.

I crave community.

I'm the person who picks up the phone and extends the invitation, but there are days when I beg God for the phone to ring.

In my prayer journal, scrawled in purple ink, it reads, *please Lord, let someone reach out to me.*

I've prayed for God to send me the group of friends I feel everyone has but me.

I've stayed up late at night, my stomach in knots, consumed with worry over the friendship that isn't quite the way it once was.

I've mustered the courage to make a call and ask if I've done something to offend. I hear the words *you haven't* and a little relief comes, but Satan still messes with my mind.

And that person who I thought I was so close to, the person who swore everything was okay, she still doesn't call.

I fret and grieve and take it personally when a friendship fades over time.

Especially the one I prayed for so long.

I feel like that 12-year-old girl staring out her bedroom window.

God what's wrong with me?

And then He reminds me, in the stillness of a dark night, that Jesus only had twelve. They were his closest companions – but of those twelve only a few shared the intimate relationship with him that I so desperately crave to share with others.

Peter, James, and John.

Those were His three.

Many times they were the only ones who got to follow Jesus and witness his miracles first-hand.

He did not let anyone follow him except Peter, James, and John the brother of James. (Mark 5:37)

After six days Jesus took Peter, James, and John with him and led them up a high mountain where they were all alone. There he was transfigured before them. His clothes became dazzling white, whiter than anyone in the world could bleach them. And there appeared before them Elijah and Moses, who were talking with Jesus. (Mark 9:2-4)

I might wish for more friends, but I never have to question whether I belong.

God says I do—even when the phone doesn't ring and the invites don't come.

I still belong even when a treasured friendship is lost.

But you belong to God, my dear children. You have already won a victory over those people, because the Spirit who lives in you is greater than the spirit who lives in the world. (1 John 4:4)

And you belong, too.

You belong to the One who understands the frustration, the hurt and the longing to be loved and accepted just as you are.

———————————————————

Jennifer Jackson Linck is the author of Bringing Home the Missing Linck: A Journey of Faith to Family, *the ebook* Trucks, Tantrums, and Trusting Him: Confessions of a Boy Mom *and* Jackson Finds His Voice, *a children's book about her son who has Childhood Apraxia of Speech.. A graduate of the University of Oklahoma, Jennifer received a bachelor's degree in journalism and spent several years working as a reporter for* The Oklahoman. *She writes about faith, adoption and special needs parenting on her blog www.jenniferjacksonlinck.com. Jennifer offers a glimmer of hope to mothers who aren't quite sure what they've gotten themselves into. Jennifer is a Texan at heart, but resides in Oklahoma with her husband, John, and their son Jackson.*

Friends Who Really Know Me
by Kathryn Shirey

"She's not doing well. You should come home." Those were the words I'd dreaded hearing. Just three weeks before my wedding date, I was summoned home because my mom had taken a turn for the worse. I made it home the night before Halloween.

She and I looked through the latest wedding gifts that had been delivered. On Halloween day we talked about last minute wedding plans, about some cookies she thought I should order for the wedding party. Then she passed away the next day. It wasn't unexpected after a lengthy battle with cancer, but that didn't lessen the grief. It didn't make the next three weeks any easier to face.

As I stayed in my hometown over the next few weeks to bury my mother, comfort my dad and then, through the grief, finalize plans for our wedding, I learned the true meaning of friendship.

Two of my best friends came and stayed with me through much of those weeks and showed love in just the ways I needed. In those weeks they taught me what it is to be a true friend.

I've been friends with these women my entire life. One I've known since we were infants in the church nursery and the other I met in kindergarten. We've been best of friends ever since. Sure, we've had a falling out or two, lost touch for some months or years along the way and haven't lived in the same town since high school, but they're still the ones I count as my closest, dearest friends.

These are the friends I've done life with. We know each other's families. I've spent time in their homes and they in mine (probably in most of the homes we've each lived in). We know what each other looks like without makeup. We've been there through the joys, heartbreaks, struggles, triumphs, weddings, births and now funerals. These women probably know me better than I know myself.

Sara dropped everything and came home to be with me. She sat and wept with me when all I could do was cry. Then she sat with me in silence when I couldn't manage words, but had cried all the tears I could cry that day. She drove all over town with me running last minute wedding errands, taking care of all the details Mom spent her last day reminding me about.

Mary came on the weekends and shared her stories of my mom. She's always been my memory keeper and she took me back to so many wonderful moments that made us smile through the tears. On a day when I just couldn't cry anymore, she took me to a funny movie and allowed me the escape and release to laugh hysterically for a couple hours.

These friends were by my side the day we buried my mother, then stood next to me in my wedding a few short weeks later.

Friendship has so many levels. We have acquaintances and casual friendships. I love those, too, and they have their place. But we need these deep friendships in our lives. We need people who know us intimately and love us deeply. Friends who will drop everything to be there in our time of need and who will celebrate joyfully with us in our triumphs. People who know the real, unmasked us. Friends who know the skeletons we hide in our closets, the fears that drive us and the subtle signs that indicate we need encouragement and prayer.

Even though mine have been lifelong friends, it's not the number of years you've known someone which makes the friendship deep. It's doing life together, going beyond the surface with each other and becoming vulnerable to share your hearts with one another. True friends are those with whom we've shared our true selves and yet love us still.

Kathryn Shirey is a wife and mom of two. She has embarked on a great journey to follow God and say "YES" to wherever He's calling her. Kathryn writes at www.kathrynshirey.com about this journey of faith - finding hope in Christ as she seeks a life transformed one step at a time.

When You Dance on Through the Awkward
by Kristin Hill Taylor

We really became friends while square dancing in October, 1998. Dressed in plaid, we were at an outing that was beyond our comfort zones. In fact, I can't remember which direction we travelled from our college campus to get to the barn where a mutual acquaintance hosted the hoe down.

Neither Jaclyn nor I really dance. But we participated in the line dances and attempted to follow the caller's instructions that night when our friendship first emerged. We swapped stories and more get-to-know-you information. We talked about immediate plans, future dreams and our young faith in God.

Befriending someone can be a risk. You may trip over your feet, but at least you won't be alone if you fall down. Neither one of us has danced many more times since then, but we've moved through many seasons in life together – usually quite in sync.

We were single college girls then. I moved away for two years after my college graduation. We began careers we believed we were created for and planned weddings to the boys who stole our hearts while we were earning our degrees. I was a journalist. She was a teacher.

But that year of swapping stories and asking for advice solidified a friendship that I'm not sure I could live without. God knew I'd need her then. And he knew I'd need her in the days to come.

When I closed the chapter on my first year of marriage and loaded up the moving truck on our anniversary, I got to say hello to living in the same town as Jaclyn. She had stayed in our college town, which was also my husband's hometown, after graduating from college the year before me.

I was so thankful to have a friend in the town that I wasn't sure I wanted to call home. Since August 2003, we've had game nights with our husbands and friends. We've shared meals and dreams around our kitchen tables. We've been in Bible studies together.

And we both wondered if we'd ever have babies after each experiencing exhausting seasons of infertility. She gave birth to a healthy baby boy in April, 2006, and birthed new hope in my life. I never saw a positive pregnancy test, but I did become a momma through three adoption processes.

We ended up having five kids in five years between us and navigated clumsily – but not alone – through motherhood and all its surprises. We quit the careers we encouraged each other to begin so we could stay at home with our kids. Our kids don't know life apart from each other. And I don't know life apart from Jaclyn.

Now I have my third child – making it six among our families – and she's returned to full-time work in a school. Thankfully, our friendship continues to adjust with the seasons life brings.

We've helped each other through surgeries, my diabetes diagnosis, the struggles of parenthood, the hard days of marriage and her desire to get back into the classroom as a teacher. We've gone to appointments with one another and to the grocery store for one another. We've celebrated birthdays together, Thanksgiving at each other's tables and Christmas with each other's families.

The richness of this friendship is ours all because we took a risk one night in a barn I can't even find anymore and opened our lives to one another. Life is certainly a dance, and friendship is one that often begins awkwardly but soon becomes beautiful.

Kristin Hill Taylor lives in Murray, Kentucky, with her husband, Greg, and three kids – Cate, Ben and Rachel. God continues to surprise her – in the best kind of way – with life looking nothing like she expected. You can follow her adventures at kristinhilltaylor.com.

An Unexpected Friendship
by Sarah Ann Goode

Our relationship didn't start like an average friendship, with a typical introduction and casual conversation. Our friendship started with tears and anger, as I did not want her in my life at all. I did not need her or appreciate her presence. Yet, the minute I held her pink squirming body in my arms for the first time, I knew she was special, and I loved my sister, Leah, wholeheartedly.

We grew up in a relationship similar to most siblings; however, being nine years older than Leah, our connection was noticeably different than the one I shared with my two younger brothers. There was something about the bond of sisterhood that was magical and enchanting. I couldn't wait to teach her everything I knew about life. After all, being nine years old, I was an expert on pretty much everything.

Being a rule follower and a quiet soul, I was not prepared for Leah's energetic and rambunctious temperament. Almost overnight, my little sister developed her own personality, a defiant spirit and a stubborn streak longer than the Mississippi River. She was headstrong and, at three years old, knew exactly what she wanted and was not afraid to make her demands known.

Surprisingly, that menacing toddler grew into a charming teenager who loved Jesus and radiated His joy. In true Leah fashion, she was bold with her faith and not ashamed of the Gospel. God was molding her into a strong woman of faith.

While we had always shared a close bond, sometime around my graduation from college and hers from high school, I realized I genuinely *liked* my baby sister. I liked Leah not just because she was my sister and we were always encouraged to make family a priority. I respected the person she had blossomed into before my very eyes. I loved that she could make me laugh like no one else, could cheer me up in an instant and could brighten even the darkest of my days with just her presence. No one else in my life shared my affection for late night junk food, understood my love of card games or kept sacred the tradition of Black Friday shopping the way Leah did. My sister was rapidly becoming a cherished friend, and whenever we said good-bye I could not wait until the next time I could see her smiling face.

When we were both married and still childless our bond grew even stronger. We understood each other, prayed for each other and spurred each other on to be more like Christ. While I never expected to be in the same season of life with someone nine years younger than me, it was such a blessing to share the everyday mundane with Leah.

Two years into my marriage the storms of life pelted me from every angle. Suddenly and without warning, there was one season of struggle after another, including my husband's battle with cancer, infertility, the long road to adoption and, most recently, the Autism diagnosis of our daughter. That's a lot to process, a lot to accept and a lot of changes to navigate.

Through every storm and every heart break, Leah stood by my side with hefty doses of laughter, tears of her own, comfort, the occasional welcomed distraction and sweet encouragement. She held my hand through it all, listened to my darkest thoughts and ministered to me in a way that few people could. She continuously guided me back to the presence of the Lord and helped heal my heart when it needed it most. She whispered words of wisdom, hope and even words of tough love into this weary soul.

I have been blessed and inspired by my sister. Like always, God knew what He was doing that warm August day when He breathed life into her and placed her in our family. He knew that baby I didn't want, that extra sibling I didn't need, would reflect His love into my life not only as my sister, but as my best friend.

Sarah Ann Goode is a perfectly imperfect wife and mother, but is thankful for the saving grace of the Lord. She shares her heart about faith, cancer survival, infertility, adoption and special needs parenting on her blog at FaithAlongtheWay.com and would be honored if you joined her on this crazy journey.

A Friend at Every Station
by Sarah Tragord

My garage is full of items to sell. Boxes scattered all around my house are being filled. Our family is on the move.

Once again it's time to say goodbye to all of the friends we have made here. And it's time to look forward to the new friends we will find at our next duty station. I find comfort during these transitions in knowing that I have a God who cares, one who has gone before me to prepare the way. (Deuteronomy 31:8) He has chosen my path, and if I trust Him I will be exactly where He wants me to be. (Jeremiah 29:11)

The blessing of being a military spouse is that I have friends all around the world. The challenge is forging friendships that are deep enough to withstand the storms of life. I want friends I can call on in the tough days, not just for a bar-b-que. Developing these types of relationships takes time, and three years at one duty station might not be enough.

Since we are never in one location too long, God has provided different friends during different seasons of my life. The season before we started a family my friends and I were more carefree. Grabbing lunch was easy and picking up the phone to catch up didn't mean putting little ones down for a nap so you could hear. These friends were typically peers and co-workers.

A few moves later we decided to start a family. God so perfectly placed a sweet friend in my path that was in the same life stage. Previously professional women, we learned together how to be stay-at-home moms—good or bad—and took many walks to the park.

Our next duty station meant another new season. Now it was time to send our first child off to school. This time God sent me a friend and a sister to share the burden of carpooling.

So here we go again. Each move starts a new season and brings hope for a new best friend. The joy that sustains me while I search for her is that Jesus is always with me. (Isaiah 41:10)

Sarah Tragord is a wife and stay-at-home mom to two very busy boys. Still a military wife, she is now pursuing a Master of Arts in Elementary Education from Liberty University. In this newest season of life Sarah doesn't have as much time for making new friends, so she is thankful for the friends she has made along the way who sustain her during these busy days.

The Church Ladies
by Gwen Williams

Several years ago, I felt empty in many areas of my life and in my everyday commitments. I knew I must prayerfully reflect about how to approach life and commitment differently. I chose to leave a church I had been attending for over eight years and started attending a church an old friend recommended. He was a pastor there and we had worked together for several years. I trusted him. I started attending, really enjoyed it and soon afterwards decided to join a women's home group through the church.

I randomly chose this group, met with the leader and felt instantly connected. We started meeting once a week and it felt like family from the very first day. There were different ages and professions represented, various lengths of time walking with the Lord and so many different needs brought before the group week after week. We shared good times and difficult times, celebrated births, grieved during loss, supported through illness and encouraged each other in our daily walk with God. And with the addition of a coffee cake and a little laughter, many times we talked far past the time the study was scheduled to end.

Our leader loved the Lord so very much and encouraged us every day. She kept us bonded through scripture and prayer requests each week and never wanted to put the spotlight on herself. Instead, she insisted on always lifting up others. Although some women came and went from the group, we had a committed few that seemed to always be there. We often had lunch and dinner dates, chatted over text messages or emails and called one another just to say hello.

We witnessed prayers answered, some delayed and some not at all. Nevertheless, we stuck by each other at every turn. I have never felt such love and support as I have felt in this group. We called ourselves the "church ladies" because we were so grounded and rooted in our faith, we were His hands and feet and were forever connected by our inspiring leader, our friend. I admired her knowledge of scripture and was in awe of her humility.

And then our group was challenged in a way we could have never imagined. Our leader received a diagnosis; the doctors said she was terminal. Our faith said God would heal, and we held to that every day. With each doctor's visit and every new protocol, we all believed God for healing. She began to weaken and needed extra care. So we started meeting at her house to give more love and support and plenty of hugs. During those months, we threw her a surprise birthday party, brought over comfort food, watched her favorite worship videos and laid hands on her, praying for a miracle. She had always been our prayer warrior and now we were hers.

One day, while planning a welcome home celebration for her after routine testing, we received news that she was soon to be on her way to Jesus. Until the very end, she loved God. And she loved us.

It's been almost a year since she went to be with her Lord, and we miss her dearly, but she would be happy to know that we are still the "church ladies", although it feels so very different. Many of us had never known each other before meeting in that group years ago, but you would never know it today. She set such a great example for me, for us. She was a woman of good character, a kind heart, a loving spirit, a tremendous love for

God, and she nurtured us in the best way. She brought us together, she made us better, she created a family.

My dear friend's verse for that season was Isaiah 41:10, *"So do not fear, for I am with you; do not be dismayed, for I am your God. I will strengthen you and help you; I will uphold you with my righteous right hand."(NIV)*

Dr. Gwen Williams is a writer, an advocate and a fan of food and travel. She is passionate about inspiring women to take steps toward developing a healthy body, soul and spirit. Gwen works with those who have experienced trauma, and feels a part of her calling is to help the hurting. She encourages self-care and empowers women through the Word of God. A contributor to various ministry blogs that encourage women in their walk with the Lord, Gwen invites you to connect with her at her website TheJourneyofHealing.com.

Investing in Friends
by Christina Parker Brown

My first weeks as a stay-at-home mom were very difficult. I was teased by my friends and ex co-workers, "Aren't you bored yet? When are you coming back to work?" I was overwhelmed caring for a newborn and I knew I needed support. I cried out to God for likeminded Christian women friends and God began answering my prayers.

I took the first step of inviting a couple of moms over for lunch from a Mommy and Me YMCA swim class, and God began designing a group of women who have now remained friends for over eighteen years. He handpicked every sister along the way. He still does.

Looking back, I realize just how big an impact these kindred spirits have made on my life. It has been a game changer. And it has been an investment. Ecclesiastes 4:9-10 talks about friendship being a good investment.

Since God began intervening through these relationships, I discovered the art of friendship and that there are three investments needed in a true friendship.

The first is to be an intentional friend. The Bible speaks of sticking closer than a brother (Proverbs 18:24). I had a Sunday school teacher that once said, "If your friend is in a fire, you need to smell like smoke." Friends encourage, work and pray for the success of their friends. I demonstrate that I am one of my friend's biggest fans through my words, my prayers and my actions.

The second investment in a friendship is to be a positive spiritual influence. The best way to point people to Christ is through my own faith. When I have a friend who is struggling, I choose to pray for them right then and there. I remember the first time a friend prayed over me. It was powerful. As a group we have experienced multiple sclerosis, cancer, alcoholism, sarcoidosis and kidney failure, divorce, infidelity, health problems, the death of parents, adoption and miscarriage. When a friend is sinning, a true friend doesn't let it go. I can show a friend love by helping her give her very best to God. Proverbs 27:17 says, "As iron sharpens iron, so a friend sharpens a friend." Prayer is a powerful way to invest in friends.

The third investment of a good friendship is to sacrifice self, sometimes at a great cost. If you call a true friend at two o'clock in the morning and tell her you need her, she doesn't ask, "So what's the problem" and then decide whether or not to come. She simply asks, "Where are you?" as she gets dressed. If my friend experiences a death in the family, I need to be there with a meal and an offer to keep her kids...even if it is inconvenient. Ecclesiastes 4:10 puts it this way, "If one falls down, his friend can help him up. But pity the man who falls and has no one to help him up!"

As this group of women grew and these investments became stronger, this circle of friendship evolved to include ministries that have gone on to bless others, including a homeschool support group for our children (now in our 18th year), a nursing home ministry where our kids are learning to be friends with people of all ages (for the last 15 years) and a monthly prayer group where we pray for our husbands, children, homes and personal struggles and successes. If you want to truly bond with other women, start praying with them and for them.

As our children grow older and begin to graduate we still meet once a month to keep the friendships alive. I believe we will keep in touch even after our husbands pass on.

I pray you are blessed with friends, but I understand it is harder for some women to make friends than others. If this is something that you struggle with, begin with prayer and cry out to God your heart's desire. God loves friendships.

Christina Parker Brown is a homeschool momma of three since 2000 and the author of AKAHomeschoolMom.com and Alphabet Smash. *Christina's passion is to encourage others to intentionally connect faith, family and fun. She always brakes for yard sales and dreams of owning chickens with her best friend and husband, Richard. You can connect with Christina on her website, AKAHomeschoolMom.com.*

My Three-Fold Friends
by Karen Sweeney-Ryall

Some of the greatest blessings in my life are my wonderful girlfriends. I am very fortunate to have several that I call my very close friends. I have had one dear friend since we were 14 years old. But I met all of my other close friends at church or in a Bible study. This isn't because I don't know or like others who don't share my faith in Jesus and the Word of God. I believe it is because sharing a love for God and having Him as the center of our lives adds an extra dimension to my friendship that I refer to as a "three-fold friendship". The connection and commitment is between me and my friend and God.

Some may not understand this, but we each are mind, body and spirit, and I am convinced that our spirit can be drawn to another or, on the other hand, repelled by another. I once had a chance encounter in a store with a woman whom I had never met before. We started chatting and by the end of our conversation we were hugging and felt a kindred bond. Toward the end of that encounter, we discovered that we were both born again Christians. I believe that our spirits connected, even before we knew anything else about each other.

But I have even more than a shared faith with my closest friends. There is not the drama and back-biting that so often occurs between women. My close friends are very aware of my strengths and my flaws, but they accept and love me as I am, and I do the same for them. We are genuine with each other. If we offer constructive criticism, we each know it is rooted in love and compassion.

About eight of my close friends were with me twelve years ago when my baby granddaughter was in critical condition in the hospital intensive care unit. It was a physically, emotionally and spiritually exhausting time, and I have rarely felt as utterly weary as I did then. For weeks I dropped my younger children off at school and then drove an hour to Children's Hospital to sit with my grandbaby and offer support to my daughter. We didn't have Facebook or even texting then so the norm was simply to call each person. Times have really changed! On any given day I simply did not have the energy to talk to more than one or two people. So I would call one of those friends and share the update and current prayer request and they would pass it on to the others. Some came to visit us in the hospital and pray with us, some made meals and brought them to my family at home and others gave rides to my children. I could feel their love, support and commitment and will forever be grateful for their faithfulness.

These precious girlfriends and I all know that we can count on one another. We can share our hearts without fear of rejection. We can be real and not fear criticism. We share conversation, prayer, dinners, fun times, retreats, worship and burdens. I am truly blessed. I believe that these special three-fold friendships are a gift from God and one of the sweet blessings of personally knowing and loving Him.

Karen Sweeney-Ryall is a speaker and author who blogs at BecomingMyBestMe.com. She is the author of Revealing Your Treasures Hidden in Darkness. Karen invites you to contact her at BecomingMyBestMe@gmail.com

Our Bathing Suits Match!
Let's be Best Friends!
by Laurie Sheffield

I love how kids can decide in a matter of minutes who is going to be their new best friend.

Watch them at the beach. A little girl sees another little girl with the same bathing suit. She walks up to introduce herself, plops down on her new friend's towel and spends the rest of the day with her new buddy...playing in the sand or water, searching for feathers, rocks and shells, declaring absolute adoration for whatever she likes. Even though this friendship has just been forged, suddenly the two little girls declare to complete strangers, "We're best friends!"

Never in a million years could I walk up to a complete stranger, plop myself down on their beach towel and ask them to be my friend...let alone express my adoration for them.

First I'd need to evaluate if we are in the same stage in life. Is she married, dating, single? Where does she stand with regard to politics? Does she go to church? And what about the whole working versus staying at home thing?

I behave as though it's an audition or job interview where one needs to "apply" to become friends. Children don't evaluate any of that. They just lean in with an "I want to know everything about you" attitude.

In fact, children find both the differences and similarities of their new friends beautiful and delightful. I watch them and notice that they almost seem to search for ways to identify similarities. "You have brown hair. That's nice. But look! We both have green eyes! Yay for green eyes!"

If we wait for "perfect fitting friends" before we reach out with an invitation we may be waiting for a long time. But if we are willing to approach friendship with the heart and curiosity of a child, meaningful relationships may look different, but they'll undoubtedly multiply more quickly.

Remarkably, I have a few of these kinds of friends. We may not appear to fit at first glance, but we do. I treasure each of these friends and how our differences outnumber our similarities.

One of my closest friends is a triathlete. I, on the other hand, have a gym membership, but can't remember the last time I used it.

Another friend recently confessed that she's dying to get a tattoo. I'd be afraid it wouldn't match my clothes!

One dear friend loves to have quiet weekends by herself to think, pray and write. I'd go insane. Another has depth and wisdom that truly inspires me...and leaves me scratching my head since she's more than a decade younger than me.

My friend who shares my love of cooking differs from me because she follows a recipe like an accountant balancing the books while I just toss in whatever is in the fridge!

Then I have a best friend that I suppose on many levels "looks" very similar to me. We're both married to doctors, teach Bible studies and speak at women's events. We're even both blondes! However, she has battled breast cancer, open heart surgery and a hip replacement all before she was out of her 40s. I've never even had a filling. I can't possibly identify with the physical struggles she's faced.

How then can we relate to each other? In each of these precious relationships we have risked being vulnerable. We don't just share information with each other; we share our lives. We feel each other's fear, sadness, joy, confusion and anger. We pray for each other. I know that I could call or text any of them and say, "I need a best friend today to pray for me...could that be you?" And it would be.

Yes, children's innocence inspires me, reminding me that making and building friendships doesn't always have to be so complicated. However, building relationships that are sweet and fulfilling does take time, intentionality and vulnerability. I think it's in sharing time with one another and being transparent that the rough edges of our differences begin to mellow and fade. We may not fit into each other's lives like pieces of a perfectly fitted jigsaw puzzle. Instead, time together, vulnerabilities shared, memories made and hearts united in prayer begin to glue us together like overlapping magazine pictures pasted onto a colorful collage. Our differences can make our relationships a little messy at times, a little challenging to navigate at others, but they also make our lives more interesting and beautiful.

Laurie Sheffield partners in ministry with two of her closest friends, Julie and Joy. Under the banner of Joy of It, they encourage unity and community among women in the body of Christ. They minister through a radio show, events and their website, JoyofIt.org. Laurie has been married to her husband Mike for over 30 years. They live in the Portland, Oregon, area.

Friends Across the Miles
by Kimberly Tucker

It was Memorial Day, 2005, as I watched her and her family pull out of the driveway. We had been dreading this day for months as we knew our time in the same church and community was coming to an end. With one final wave goodbye, we both cried and their van turned the corner and was out of sight.

I remember standing in the driveway thinking "What do I do now?" We wouldn't be taking that morning run the next day, going to choir rehearsal together that Wednesday night or planning that next women's event at church.

Our husbands had served on staff together at the same church for the past six years, but Kay and I had done so much more than that. We had raised our kids side-by-side, prayed together regularly, led our women's ministry, sang in a trio and become the best of friends. Now God had called her husband to pastor a church in Arizona. *Arizona!* That was 900 miles away from where I lived in Texas. How could we keep a close friendship going 900 miles apart? But we did!

Kay and I have continued to encourage each other, speak truth into each other's lives, shoulder each other's burdens and enjoy our friendship, even while living 900 miles apart. I can't say it's been easy. In fact, it has been challenging. We've not only had to change the way we do friendship, but we've had to grow up individually.

We have kept our friendship vibrant by talking via the telephone on a regular basis, keeping each other informed of what's going on in our lives. But it's not just the weekly phone calls that have kept us connected. We've continued to be invested, to care and to pray for one another. Even as life has taken us in different directions, Kay and I have stayed interested in what God is doing in each other's life. For six years we led somewhat parallel lives and devoted ourselves to many of the same pursuits. But because we now live in different places and invest heavily in different churches and personal ministries, we find ourselves pursuing different dreams and struggling with different dilemmas. The temptation is to believe you no longer have enough in common to maintain a thriving relationship. But honestly it's because we have *less* in common that we have become more giving toward one another and have learned what it really means to love another...even when there is no immediate benefit for oneself. We've had to practice Philippians 2:4, which says, "do not merely look out for your own interests, but also the interests of others."

Kay encouraged me to continue my education so I could pursue a counseling ministry and I encouraged her to invest more heavily in her writing and speaking ministry. We have believed in each other's potential and dreams, and we've pushed each other to achieve those dreams. I have had the honor of traveling with Kay as her ministry assistant, and those ministry events have taken us all over the United States and to Japan and Canada.

While we enjoy traveling together, it's been important to me that we also visit in each other's home and just "hang out" together when possible. We also try to attend the big events in each other's lives. Kay was my right hand woman at my daughter's wedding, helping me do all those little things you do just before a big church wedding. I attended her daughter's high school graduation. I flew to Arizona on our shared birthday (now that's a sweet bonus!) to help her celebrate her 50th with a big party with her best gal pals. And that same spring, Kay took the time, effort and money to join me in Georgia to celebrate my walk across the stage as I received my doctorate in counseling.

My dear friend and I don't always know each other's daily routines like we once did. And we actually connect on the telephone even less often than we did initially after she moved. But we have committed to a close, intimate relationship regardless of the distance. We support each other and, when we can, we take the time and travel those 900 miles to be there for each other and our families. We make the relationship a priority. It is not *the* priority of our lives, but it is *a* priority. We have watched God work in each other's lives and see us through a very difficult time of adjustment. Kay and I both know that we can count on each other and that, when needed, we will continue to be there for each other. Physical miles do separate us, but we have willingly and intentionally kept our hearts close.

Dr. Kimberly Tucker is a licensed Christian counselor in Garland, Texas. She is also heavily invested in the ministries of her church, Northrich Baptist Church in Richardson, Texas, where her husband Brent is the pastor. She continues to lead her church's women's ministry and mentors young women and teen girls. Kimberly has three grown children and two grandchildren.

Part 3

Between Us Friends

a study guide

Wouldn't it be fun to talk about the ideas and stories in this book with a few friends? Whether you've known each other for years or you just met, the material in this little book could make for sweet conversation among friends.

You could gather in a backyard with a tall pitcher of lemonade between you and children playing noisily all around. Or you could sneak off to a coffee shop, take a corner booth and exchange thoughts over piping hot beverages to fit your different tastes. Hey, you could even Skype, share a conference call or open a Facebook page for group discussion, if life has taken you to different corners of the world.

This little study guide offers:

- a simple reading plan

- occasional scriptures to read

- questions for you to toss around with your group

- space for you to write your answers

- a place to record prayer requests from your friends

- and room to jot down insights gained around the table.

If you choose to use the study guide, make it work for you. *It's organized for four discussion sessions,* but you can always rearrange it so that you can complete it in two or three if necessary. Each participant will need a book, and it would probably be best if one or two of you took the responsibility of leadership, deciding when and where you'll meet and navigating the conversation. Also, it might be best to keep your group size to between three and eight. But you're welcome to override that suggestion if your basket of friends overflows. Enjoy!

Session One

Reading Plan:

Before meeting for group discussion, read the following:

Just for Fun

Look for old photos of you and friends from your past...childhood, teen years, college, etc. Share one or two with the group and talk briefly about the friends in the pictures.

Table Talk with Friends

1. Kay wrote on page 4, "A friend is someone who speaks into your life, and you speak into hers on a mutual basis." Later she asserted that, "friendship is an ongoing conversation." How do these definitions help you to better understand the unique dynamics of friendship in contrast with other relationships you may have?

2. What are some of the parts of the conversation between friends that are most important to you? Why? (page 5)

3.   Which of the three essentials Kay mentioned on page 8 is most difficult for you: courage, initiative or personal responsibility? Discuss how each of these is needed in order to develop healthy and beneficial friendships.

4.   Explain what a Red Delicious Apple friend is. What is the basis for this type of friendship?

5.   Kay shared that she and her hairdresser Marilyn have a Red Delicious Apple friendship. Share about a friendship you have that began when you both realized you had something in common.

6.   Why did Kay insist that Red Delicious Apple friendships are important for us to have even if they may not be the deepest or most treasured relationships? (see page 12) Why do you agree or disagree?

7.   What do you think about Kay's suggestion for *how* to begin a Red Delicious Apple friendship? What are some of the reasons we neglect to "invite her?" Discuss among your friends how you could each put this tip into practice in the near future.

8. On page 17, Kay listed some of the "common pests, bruises and diseases" that sometimes cause our Red Delicious Apple friendships to "go bad." *Keeping the focus on your own responsibility*, discuss honestly how you have allowed one of these or another malady to injure a friendship in the past. What did you learn from that experience?

9. List some of the things that keep women from making new friends. Discuss among you which hindrance trips *you* up the most.

10. In "Finding a Friendship Lost," Valerie Sisco shared about reuniting with a lost childhood friend. Have you reconnected with a childhood friend in recent years? Share your experience briefly. What was most interesting about that reconnection?

11. Bridget Bareither shared in her essay, "Letting My Guard Down," that she had to "let my guard down" in order to even meet new friends. What do you think she meant by "let my guard down"? Discuss why it is so hard to do that.

12. Bridget also mentioned several gatherings she attended in order to meet new friends. Where have you gone or what have you done in order to meet new people? Be sure to list new ideas for where to meet new friends as you discuss this question.

13. In "God-Gift Friendships," Becky Keife wrote, "I needed a new inner circle. A day-in-day-out friend to walk through the ins and outs of motherhood together." While it is easier to keep up with long distance friends now because of cell phones and social media, do you think it is important to have a circle of local friends with whom you "do life?" Why or why not?

14. Even if you already have plenty of friends during this season of life, do you think it is important to stay open to new friendships? Why or why not?

Prayer Requests Shared Among Friends:

Insights Gained from Discussion:

Goals:

Next meeting date and time:

Session Two

Reading Plan:

Before meeting for group discussion, read the following:

Just for Fun

Take the following supplies to the group meeting:

- enough green apples for each person to have one

- a Sharpie marker for each person

- a paring knife for each person (have each woman bring one from home)

- optional: the remaining ingredients and recipe for baking an apple pie or crisp

As you discuss question #2, have each person write on their apple the things that sour the conversation between friends. Then, as you discuss question #7 have each woman peel her apple. See who can peel her apple in one long strip of apple peel! You could all dice your apples, put them in a large storage bag with a sprinkle of lemon juice and bake an apple pie or crisp together halfway through the session. Then you could enjoy it after the remaining discussion questions.

Table Talk with Friends

1. Do you agree or disagree with Kay's theory that we all have a few friends that we don't really enjoying spending too much time with? Explain.

2. In your own experience, what are some of the ways a conversation between two friends can "sour", causing you to distance yourself?

3. Without naming names or giving details, do you currently have Green Delicious Apple friendships due to soured conversation? How have you been treating that friend(s)? Why?

4. Read John 12:1-8.

    - What did Judas say in this scenario that may have been sour to Jesus?

    - Why would those remarks be offensive to Him?

    - In addition to Judas' remarks being hurtful, why else might Jesus have been tempted to treat Judas differently? (see verse 4)

    - How did Jesus treat Judas in this passage?

5. Read Matthew 26:45-50.

- What is taking place in this passage?

- How did Judas set up the betrayal? He betrayed Jesus with a _____.

- What did Jesus call Judas in this scenario? Why do you think that is significant?

6. Read Hebrews 4:14-16.

- Do you think Jesus struggled with His relationship with Judas? Discuss your answer.

- What do you learn from Jesus' relationship with Judas about how to relate to your Green Delicious Apple friends?

- What hope does Hebrews 4:14-16 give you in your Green Delicious Apple friendships?

7. Discuss some of the ways you can sweeten a Green Delicious Apple friendship, both Kay's ideas and your own.

8. What responsibility do you think you have toward your Green Delicious Apple friends, if any?

9. In "Transparency in Friendship," Chris Adams described how she was surprised by the transparency of her older friend. Why is transparency so important in friendship? How difficult is it for you to be transparent?

10. In Cindy Dykes' essay "Heartbreaking Needs, Heartwarming Friends" she disclosed that a shared difficult family situation drew her into friendship with two women. But she hinted that the same situation perhaps caused some other women to pull away from her. Have you experienced a difficult situation that both divided you from some friends and drew you closer to others? Share without disclosing information that would wound others.

11. Jennifer Jackson Linck shared some of her deepest insecurities in the area of friendship. She found solace in the fact that Jesus also only invested in a small number of friends. What makes you feel insecure about making and keeping friends? How does Jesus' example of friendship encourage you?

12. In "Friends Who Really Know Me," Kathryn Shirey shared how two dear friends stepped in with persistence and great love after her mother died just before her wedding. Have you ever had friends who showed similar determination by pressing in when you needed it? If you were in Kathryn's shoes, what would you hope for from friends in order to feel safe and encouraged in their love? Could you provide that to someone else?

Prayer Requests Shared Among Friends:

Insights Gained from Discussion:

Goals:

Next meeting date and time:

Session Three

Reading Plan:

Before meeting for group discussion, read the following:

1 Samuel 18:1-9; 19:1-7; 20:1-42

Just for Fun

Put the Scrabble tiles for the letters A,P,P,L,E,S,G,O,L & D in a brown paper bag. At the group meeting have each woman draw a letter. Each woman will then explain the characteristic of a Golden Delicious Apple friend beginning with the letter she pulled out of the bag.

As a bonus, encourage each woman to lead your group through an exercise in which you all learn to put into practice that characteristic. For instance, a woman who draws "L" could tell a joke for levity, a woman who draws "G" could tell how she experienced grace from God by sharing her salvation testimony or a woman who draws "S" could help the women make a list of standards they could establish in a friendship. You might want to do this exercise just before you answer question #4.

Table Talk with Friends

1. Although you can easily find Golden Delicious apples in your grocery store most any time, what about their origin makes them significant?

2. How would you describe a Golden Delicious Apple friendship to someone who hasn't read this chapter?

3. Why do you think Kay used Proverbs 25:11 to explain the unique characteristics of a Golden Delicious Apple friendship? (Page 31)

4. Looking over the acrostic APPLES of GOLD, what seems to be the common denominator in all of the characteristics of this friendship? Explain.

5. If you have a Golden Delicious Friend or two, share with the group what that friend contributes to your life that is of the most value to you.

6. If you have a Red Delicious Apple friendship that you would like to prayerfully move toward a Golden Delicious Apple friendship, how would you start? What responsibility would you take to make your relationship golden?

7. After reading the story of David and Jonathan's friendship in 1 Samuel, what characteristics of the Golden Delicious Apple friendship do you see in this relationship?

8. Read John 15:13. How does Jesus describe the greatest love in this statement? How do you see that characteristic in a Golden Delicious Apple friendship?

9. In "When You Dance on Through the Awkward," Kristin Taylor describes a close, long-lasting friendship that resulted from an awkward evening. What awkward moments or situations can you think of that friends may need to press through in order to build a sustaining friendship? What blessings often lie on the other side of awkward?

10. Sarah Ann Goode wrote in "An Unexpected Friendship" that she has developed a cherished friendship with her younger sister. What friendship has taken you by surprise? Why is that friendship so sweet?

11. In "A Friend at Every Station," author Sarah Tragord praises God for providing friends even though her husband's military career requires that they move often. When you meet someone whom you may only live near for a limited time, do you still reach out in friendship? Why or why not?

Prayer Requests Shared Among Friends:

Insights Gained from Discussion:

Goals:

Next meeting date and time:

Session Four

Reading Plan:

Before meeting for group discussion, read the following:

Just for Fun

This week we're focusing on the differences between unhealthy and healthy friendships. Encourage each woman to bring a favorite healthy snack to share and the recipe if it's homemade. Encourage women to bring enough to share at the meeting and separately portioned containers of her snack for each woman to take home. Examples would be granola, yogurt, raisins, fruit parfaits, healthy cookies, veggie sticks or even bottled water.

Table Talk with Friends

1. Kay describes the unhealthy codependent friendship as one that is both sweet and sticky. List what might seem sweet about such a friendship. Then list what makes such a relationship sticky.

    <u>Sweet:</u>

Sticky:

2.   Kay said that her codependent friendship must have grieved the Lord. Why would a codependent friendship be offensive to God according to the following scriptures?

     • Exodus 20:2-6 –

     • Deuteronomy 6:5 –

     • Romans 1:21-25 –

     • Galatians 1:10 –

3.   Why do you think the following characteristics of a healthy friendship are so important?

     •   *autonomy* or the ability to pursue separate interests and relationships

     •   *freedom* to keep information private, to make plans apart from one another and to pull back some

- *relationships* with other people that are enjoyable, fulfilling and separate

- *personal boundaries* that are respected and not crossed

4. Over the past weeks, since you began reading this book and exploring the relationship of friendship, how have you challenged yourself to grow or change? What positive steps have you made?

5. In the chapter "What's in Your Basket?" Kay presents four friendship challenges. Which will you take on seriously this next week? Explain your plans and ask for prayer support.

6. In "The Church Ladies," Gwen Williams shared about a friendship with a mentor that multiplied into an enduring group of friends. Do you have a group of friends or are your friendships mostly separate relationships? How do you feel about this?

7. Christina Brown said in "Investing in Friends" that there are three necessary investments in friendships. Discuss each investment and the fruit it could produce.

8. In "My Three-Fold Friends" Karen Sweeney-Ryall shared how her friends came through for her in a variety of ways when her granddaughter was critically ill. How have your friends come through for you in difficult times?

9. Author Laurie Sheffield wrote about the differences that sometimes prevent us from initiating friendships, but ultimately make our relationships more beautiful. Are you friends with someone who is beautifully different from you? How does that friendship make your life richer?

10. Kim Tucker shared how she has kept a friendship alive and vibrant over hundreds of miles that separate her from her friend in "Friends Across the Miles." What do you think are the keys to sustaining close friendships with women who no longer live near you?

Prayer Requests Shared Among Friends:

Insights Gained from Discussion:

Goals:

About the Author

Born and raised in Georgia, Kay Harms and her husband James now call Arizona home. Because her husband has pastored churches in four states and they've served for almost twelve years in a military town, Kay has friends all over the world.

Kay has a degree in journalism from the University of Georgia. She speaks at women's events around the country, mentors women and teaches weekly Bible studies at her church.

Kay has authored several Bible studies, including *Joseph – Keeping a Soft Heart in a Hard Place* and *Satisfied...at Last!*

The Harms have two adult children, Daniel and Abigail, who keep them grounded and humble.

Connect with Kay at kayharms.com, on Facebook at www.facebook.com/official.kayharms and on Instagram at @kay_harms.

About Kay's Bible Studies

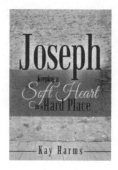

In *Joseph: Keeping a Soft Heart in a Hard Place*, learn how to face life's hurtful situations the way Joseph did in Genesis 37-50. Find healing for your broken heart and courage to love again. Find hope to replace despair.

The 7-week, verse-by-verse Bible study includes an optional zero-week and focuses on the heart of this amazing man. Optional DVDs are available only at KayHarms.com.

Every woman is a hungry woman. We're hungry for love, significance, purpose and security. Learn practical and biblical principles for how to be fully satisfied through a daily diet of the Bread of Life.

Satisfied...at Last! is a 6-week Bible study with discussion questions, appropriate for group or individual study.

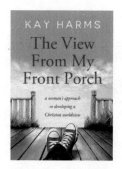

This 4-week study helps you build a biblical worldview so that you can relate to the world around you the way God does. *The View from My Front Porch* addresses a current topic from a distinctly feminine perspective.

Kay's books are available at Amazon.com, BarnesandNoble.com & KayHarms.com/books. But for group discounts, inquire through email: admin@kayharms.com.